'J'FOR

JOHNNIE

This edition published in Great Britain in 2015
by
Laundry Cottage Books
Shropshire, England
01952 223931
Email: cenneach@westcoast13.wanadoo.co.uk

© John Trotman 2011

First Edition published in 2011

ISBN 978-0-9550601-7-5

Proofreading & editing by
Sue Browning Editing and Proofreading

Printed and bound in England by
Printondemandworldwide.com

'J' for Johnnie

John Trotman grew up in the pre-war England of the 1920s and 30s. When war came he joined the RAF and flew seventy operational missions over Germany and occupied Europe in the Wellington & Mosquito bombers of 150 & 692 Squadrons, including the last two raids of the war carried out by Bomber Command in Europe before peace once more settled upon the land.

This is John's own story.

Flight Lieutenant
John Trotman DFC & Bar

Laundry Cottage Books

Laundry Cottage Books
Publishing
Laundry Cottage
Shawbirch Road
Admaston, Wellington
Shropshire, TF5 0AD
Tel: 01952 223931

Email: cenneach@westcoast13.wanadoo.co.uk

Laundry Cottage Books is an independent publisher which endeavours to keep alive the memory of those people who have given so much for our freedom by recording and publishing previously untold stories in its First and Second World War biography series.

Titles in this series published by Laundry Cottage Books

'J' for Johnnie
John Trotman, DFC*
ISBN 978-0-9550601-7-5
The story of Flt Lt John Trotman, DFC*, pilot
RAF Bomber Command

Another Dawn Another Dusk
Kenneth Ballantyne
ISBN 978-0-9550601-3-7
The story of WO Trevor Bowyer, DFC,ISM rear gunner
RAF Bomber Command

All the Things You Are
Kenneth Ballantyne
ISBN 978-0-9550601-4-4
Twelve short stories from the Home Front in WW2

First Wave
Kenneth Ballantyne
ISBN 978-0-9550601-6-8
The story of WO Reg Payne, wireless operator
RAF Bomber Command

Holding the Line
Kenneth Ballantyne
ISBN 978-0-9550601-8-2

[Publication due summer 2016]
The story of Sapper Rowland Hill
on the Western Front during WW1

The D-Day Dodger
Albert F Darlington
ISBN 978-0-9550601-2-0
The story of Private Albert Darlington,
Ox & Bucks Light Infantry – Italian campaign

The Journey
Kenneth Ballantyne
[Title no longer in print]

Acknowledgements

I am particularly grateful to my publisher, Kenneth Ballantyne of Laundry Cottage Books, who has encouraged and helped me to revisit my original manuscript and add to it by recording some of my seventy operational missions in more detail, as well as describing some of the wider events which were taking place around me during the war. Without Kenneth, this second edition would not have seen the light of day and the story of the immense courage of my crews on two squadrons would not have been told. I am also grateful to him for kindly allowing me to reproduce the text from *Another Dawn Another Dusk* as the first paragraph of Chapter 5.

My sincere thanks to all those many and varied people who have kindly helped me when I was writing this book and/or have provided and permitted me to use their illustrations and photographs. I have credited these pictures in the text where they appear. All other photographs are from my private collection.

My thanks are also due to Sue Browning of Sue Browning Editing and Proofreading for kindly keeping my text within the bounds of established English grammar, spelling and punctuation whilst guiding the flow of my story through the pitfalls of writing. If I have dabbled with the manuscript after Sue returned it, I and my publishers accept full responsibility for any consequential errors.

Finally, but certainly not least, my enduring thanks and gratitude go to my loving wife, Olwen. Not only did she encourage me to write my story in the first place, but she conspired with Kenneth to ensure that I revisited the text and wrote this much fuller account.   John Trotman April 2015

This book is dedicated to my wife, Olwen,
our sons and daughter, and
to all those comrades in arms
who gave their all
for love of country and freedom

Foreword

This meticulous but direct account evoked a picture of the Second World War that some readers will know inside out but others will be picking up at one or two removes. There is plenty of specialist information about different aircraft and their handling capacities, which will please aviation enthusiasts, but there is also a strong human-interest element, following the progress of an ordinary airman through the ranks – via Cranwell, Shawbury, Pershore, and Graveley – until he has earned a commission and a DFC and Bar, which will entertain any reader.

There are tragic moments too – such as when a crew member dies, perhaps through the fault of the pilot – and personal revelations – when war stress leads to John's marriage breakdown, or his sister's tragic death from septicaemia after the birth of her child. But there are also humorous moments, such as when a wild American called Tex shoots down whisky bottles at Betty's Dive in York. Through all this comes the modest voice of a man determined to speak the truth, plainly.

The list of German cities John Trotman flew sorties to is startling: Cologne, Hanover, Kamen, Nuremberg, Duisburg, Karlsruhe, Mannheim, Erfurt, Kassel, Bremen, Dessau, Hamburg, Munich, Husum, Berlin, Kiel, and Ludwigshafen. The excitement and skill required to drop mines at the U-boat 'haven' in Saint-Nazaire in France is graphically recounted.

John Gillespie Magee's poem 'High Flight' is a fitting introduction to the spirit of the book:

'Oh I have slipped the surly bonds of earth.
And while with silent lifting mind I've trod

The High untrespassed sanctity of space,
Put out my hand, and touched the face of God!'

But for me, the most spine-tingling sentence is the humble prayer squeezed in modestly towards the end: *'I hope that when the day of reckoning comes, I may be forgiven for causing the deaths of so many people during the war, and given credit for some of the good things I have done in my life since.'*

A truly awe-inspiring personal biography, from a man of exceptional integrity.

Mike Wilmott – Shrewsbury Words.

Contents

Acknowledgements

Foreword

Preface

High Flight by John Gillespie Magee

Chapter

Author's Preface to the First Edition

As a result of a broken pelvis and a later attack of bronchial pneumonia, my wife Olwen encouraged me to write an autobiography to keep my mind occupied in the long winter evenings. Though lacking in computer experience, this was achieved – with bouts of frustration, including losing much of the text, learning the techniques of moving text, resizing pictures and so on. I hope the result will be satisfactory and show my sincere endeavours.

Publisher's Preface to this Edition

In his customary, ever-so modest manner, John Trotman recounted his wartime RAF years in the first edition of this book in a way which inevitably left his readers feeling that his remarkable record of seventy operational missions over two tours and five years of war were somehow incidental to his RAF service of thrills and spills. He simply did not realise that they wanted to know so much more about his part in those operations. John had not wanted anyone to think that he was, as they say in the RAF, shooting a line.

John Trotman was awarded the Distinguished Flying Cross, and was then awarded a bar to that DFC; he does not need to shoot a line, his record speaks for itself. John's entire operational service was pitched against the enemy in Germany and occupied Europe. For RAF Bomber Command crews, there was no more dangerous a theatre of war nor one where the life expectancy was so short; even subalterns serving in the trenches of the Western Front during the Great War were expected to live longer than their sons who would serve as Bomber Command aircrews over Europe some twenty-five years later.

What John has done in this second edition of 'J' for Johnnie is to share some greater detail of his operational missions and particularly what his feelings were at the time. The result is a much rounder personal account of John Trotman, the young pilot of a Wellington bomber with No.150 Squadron during 1942/43 and then as the older, experienced pilot of the immensely fast, manoeuvrable and lethal Mosquito fighter-bomber in 1944/45 with No.692 Squadron. His operational tours were interspersed with periods as an instructor, which he found often proved to be every bit as dangerous as operations against the enemy.

John survived and then set about building a life in post-war Britain. Part of that particular struggle necessitated the agonising decision to sell his wartime medals, Log Books and congratulatory telegram from Air Chief Marshal Harris on the award of his first DFC. Years later, John, now widowed, would meet and fall in love with Olwen, his physiotherapist, who would help him to track down and recover those medals from the other side of the world.

This is not a book to be missed. It is the fascinating first-hand account of a remarkable man and his wartime service.

Laundry Cottage Books
8th May 2015
70th Anniversary of VE Day

High Flight

Oh! I have slipped the surly bonds of Earth
And danced the skies on laughter-silvered wings;
Sunward I've climbed, and joined the tumbling mirth
Of sun-split clouds, – and done a hundred things
You have not dreamed of – wheeled and soared and swung
High in the sunlit silence. Hov'ring there
I've chased the shouting wind along, and flung
My eager craft through footless halls of air...
Up, up the long, delirious burning blue
I've topped the wind-swept heights with easy grace
Where never lark, or ever eagle flew –
And while with silent, lifting mind I've trod
The high untrespassed sanctity of space,
Put out my hand, and touched the face of God.
John Gillespie Magee, Jr

(reproduced by kind permission of *This England* magazine)

John Gillespie Magee, Jr was born in Shanghai in 1922 to an English mother and a Scottish-Irish-American father. On 3rd September 1941, Magee flew a high-altitude test flight in a Spitfire V and was struck with the inspiration for a poem. In a letter to his parents he commented: "I am enclosing a verse I wrote the other day. It started at 30,000 feet and was finished soon after I landed." On the back was his poem 'High Flight'. Magee was killed in a mid-air collision over Lincolnshire on 11th December 1941, just three months after writing it. After his death, the poem was published and rapidly became world famous. It is widely regarded as the finest poem about flying ever written.

CHAPTER 1
The formative years

1921 was a notable year, in which a number of well-known people were born: Maureen O'Hara, Harry Secombe, Peter Ustinov, Donald Campbell – and me, to name but a few. I was born on the 9th September 1921, in Winchester Hospital, at 8 o'clock in the morning; why in a hospital I never found out. In those days, children were normally born at home, unless there were extenuating circumstances: perhaps it was because my mother was 36 years old when I was born, which, although not unusual now, was then.

My father, Percival Vincent Povey Trotman, a Gloucestershire man, was born in Wotton-under-Edge. He worked as a chauffeur for a number of years for a gentleman named Colonel Ucter Knox, who had a small estate at Holt Hatch, just outside the village of Bentley, which is near Farnham in Surrey. Before the First World War, dressed in a long overcoat and chauffeur's hat, my father would drive the Colonel in an upright Daimler car, in which the driver sat in the front with a roof over his head but no side windows.

On one occasion, he drove the Colonel to Dover, where the car was loaded by crane onto the cross-channel ferry, off-loaded at Calais, and then they proceeded through France and Switzerland to Italy. Father reckoned that he had to repair a puncture every 100 miles because the poor state of the roads. He concluded that the purpose of the trip was to allow the Colonel to reconnoitre the defences and other preparations in various countries in Europe prior to the onset of the Great War.

When the War broke out, my father enlisted in the Army and served in Iraq, or Mesopotamia as it was still called at that time, in the RAMC as an ambulance driver. At the end of the war, he returned to England and his employment with the Colonel at Holt Hatch.

My mother, Susan Helen, was the eldest daughter of a builder, John Horton, in Eastbourne. He built rows of Victorian back-to-back houses in the town, which he sold or rented out. When he died, he left the house he lived in to his wife and gave the remaining rented properties to the chapel. In due course, a hall was built in his memory in the locality, but over the years, the area deteriorated, the houses and the hall were demolished and the council built on the land.

After marrying my father, my mother joined him at Holt Hatch and became housekeeper to the Colonel. We lived in a tied cottage adjacent to the garage, where two cars were kept, and at a very young age one day, I decided to develop my artistic talents by painting one of the cars with paint I had found in the garage. On discovering the results of my endeavours, my father desperately set to work with turpentine and petrol and fortunately managed to salvage the situation.

Adjacent to the cottage was Alice Holt Forest, and I loved to go exploring in the woods, much to my parents' great concern. Amazingly, I never got lost!

At 5, I attended Bentley Church of England School, and was taken by my sister Marjory, who was five years older than me. In order to get to school we followed a footpath for a quarter of a mile, crossed the local two-track railway line at the unmanned local level-crossing, walked some distance across a field to a wooden bridge crossing the river Wey, up an unmade road to the A31 main road, which we crossed, traversed some common land, eventually arriving at school after a total walk of

1½ miles. The same journey was travelled every school day, except in really inclement weather, when the river would flood, in which case we would have to go via the roads, adding an extra half a mile.

Bentley village school consisted of just three classrooms, containing, respectively, 5-7, 8-9 and 11-13-year-old children. The headmaster, Mr Beeken, did everything possible to ensure that every child in his school, on leaving, was capable in mathematics, reading, and writing, and had a reasonable knowledge of British history and world geography. Additionally, he encouraged sports for both boys and girls. On leaving school, pupils could opt for menial jobs, attend the local very good technical college, which offered a wide range of practical subjects and worked in conjunction with local employer apprenticeship schemes, or go to a grammar school, of which there were four within reasonable travelling distance.

The railway station at Bentley was a junction for a local branch line to Bordon and, as a result, there was some locomotive shunting done as the branch line train came into Bentley station then changed over to a branch line platform. Another lad and I haunted the station and at last persuaded the driver of the branch line's little tank engine to let us ride with him on the footplate as the shunting took place – a great thrill. We also experimented with placing halfpenny pieces on the railway lines. These would be squashed to the size of a penny, which we would then put into the chocolate vending machine on the platform and obtain penny bars of chocolate. I sometimes think that the children of today have no idea what true fun growing up is.

At 14, my sister Marjory went as a children's assistant nurse to look after the children of an army colonel who was stationed at the time in Aldershot, but who subsequently took his family to India, and my sister went with them. I have to say that my sister and I were not close, but her presence and help from time to time were comforting. I didn't see her again until 1943. At 11 years of age I sat the entrance exam for the Alton Grammar School, but failed to pass. I was 'a late developer'.

My mother was determined that I should have a decent education, so I was sent as a fee-paying pupil to Aldershot County High School, a local grammar school that took a limited number of fee-paying pupils. Fees were £5 per term, plus books and uniform. In those days, that was quite a commitment, bearing in mind that the national average wage was between £2-10s-0d and £3-0s-0d per week.

About this time, Colonel Knox died and my father and mother were forced to obtain alternative employment. We moved to the centre of Bentley village, to a house aptly named *Crossroads*, where my father set up a garage, taxi and private hire business. To supplement their income, my mother set up a tearoom together with a bed and breakfast business.

Next door to *Crossroads* was the local Memorial Hall used for all community functions. The local Boy Scouts met there regularly, and my mother felt I should join. Accordingly, I attended a Scouts' meeting, but as the Scout Master was ill, his stand-in was none other than Lord Baden-Powell, the founder of the Scout movement, who lived locally. To my mother's great disgust and dismay, I never attended another meeting. The Memorial Hall was also used by the village school to put on plays and I remember acting as a convict in one play, my trousers and coat being covered in broad black arrows. My performance could not have been too bad, though, as I remember that the audience clapped quite enthusiastically.

I travelled to school at Aldershot daily by train from Bentley station, leaving my bike in the station bicycle rack all day. It was always there when I got back. The bicycle had been a birthday present from my parents, and had cost the princely sum of £4-19s-6d. Occasionally, when I missed the train, I would cycle to school. On these occasions, as I left home, a local Courage brewery lorry would pass the house, travelling from Alton to London, and I would tuck in behind it, being pulled along by the slipstream at quite a fast speed. This nearly resulted in disaster when one day, as I tucked in behind the brewery lorry, I felt a touch on the shoulder, only to realise that the lorry was towing a trailer. I extricated myself in the nick of time. It was a shock and a lesson learnt!

At school, I became friendly with Johnnie Rolland and Ken Holman, both from army families, Bill Bradshaw, whose father ran a fish and chip shop, and Norman Powell, whose father was a bus conductor. I would meet Johnnie and Ken again in very different circumstances during the war. The four of us vied for top position in our form in all subjects, except Latin, in which I was a poor scholar. Aldershot County High School was a grammar school which took in pupils from all backgrounds, but after attending for two years, it was reserved for girls only, and all we boys were sent to the newly opened Farnborough Grammar School. Here, the headmaster and teachers were all male and there was a high standard of teaching. Unlike today, teachers moved from classroom to classroom, pupils remaining where they were, except for lessons in the physics and chemistry laboratories.

Going to Farnborough meant travelling by train to Aldershot, then catching a double-decker school bus from the station to the new school. En route, the bus passed the entrance to the Farnborough Aerodrome and almost immediately adjacent was a Catholic girls' school surrounded by a high wall. As boys, we tried to ensure we were positioned on the top deck of the bus as we passed the high wall, over which we could see the attractive-looking girls. On one occasion all the boys were in position on one side of the top deck as the bus rounded the corner, leaving the poor bus driver desperately fighting to control the bus, which had become lopsided. He stopped the bus and gave us a piece of his mind, in no uncertain terms.

I was reaching the age of puberty, and rather fancied a girl attending Aldershot County High School. We arranged a date on a Saturday to meet and go to the cinema. I cycled furiously towards Bentley station to catch a train to meet her at Aldershot, but at the bottom of a steep hill the mudguard of my bicycle fouled the front wheel, sending me flying over the handlebars, suffering cuts and minor concussion, and a broken tooth which has never been repaired. Fortunately, a lady pushing a pram was passing at the time and took me to a local house and telephoned my father, who came and rescued me. Needless to say, I didn't keep the date or get a second chance.

In June 1938, I sat the matriculation exam and obtained distinctions in English Language, English Literature, Mathematics, History and Geography but failed in Physics. I re-sat Physics, but still didn't pass. The question of going on to university didn't arise, as in those days going to university was for the well-to-do and those awarded a grant.

By now, the storm clouds of war were beginning to appear over Europe. In March, Hitler occupied Austria, followed by the occupation of Czechoslovakia in September. It was at this time that Prime Minister Neville Chamberlain returned from a meeting with Hitler, waving a piece of paper in the air, and stating that there would be "Peace in our time".

During 1938, a series of coastal radar stations had been built, particularly along the south coast of England, and at the same time, RAF Bomber Command was busily building up its strength of bombers. These included Blenheims, Hampdens, Whitleys and Wellingtons, though, with the exception of the Wellington, they were already obsolete when compared with the bombers of the German Luftwaffe.

In January 1939, I started to look for work. There was still relatively high unemployment and jobs were hard to find, particularly if you had only academic qualifications. I filled in time helping my mother in her business waiting on tables and helping my father by driving taxis. Because my father was in the motor business, I had been able to drive cars from the age of 13, though not on public highways. Finally, on my own initiative, I got a job as a plumber's mate, working for a company fitting central heating in the army barracks in Aldershot. My old headmaster heard what I was doing, was shocked and arranged for me to work in a sports shop in Aldershot, but I found the hours of working all day on Saturdays with a half day off on Wednesdays not to my liking. Accordingly, I found a job with a water company in Farnham, which was nearer to my home, and working half days on Saturdays instead of all day suited my social arrangements much better. Around this time, I had the idea that I might take up accountancy in view of the fact that I found I could easily understand ledgers, billing, receipts, invoicing, etc.

911 25hp

An early Daimler
[courtesy Daimler Motors]

CHAPTER 2
Joining up

As 1939 dawned, Britain seriously started to rearm, and then in September, Germany invaded Poland, with the immediate result that both Britain and France declared that we were in a state of war with Germany. I well remember Neville Chamberlain's speech announcing that we were at war. Subsequently, Germany invaded Denmark and Norway, where British Forces were sent to help the Norwegians but unfortunately had later to withdraw.

The British Expeditionary Force (BEF) had embarked for France to support French forces and four squadrons of Hurricane fighters had been sent to France, leaving twenty-two squadrons in England for the defence of Britain. Bomber Command had fifty-five squadrons mostly consisting of old aircraft, as already mentioned, and sent a number of Blenheims and Fairey Battles to France.

At home, everyday living conditions remained pretty much the same and this so-called 'phoney' war lasted into 1940. Prior to this time, in early 1939, the Government had announced conscription, which meant that young men of twenty and twenty-one would be called up for compulsory service in the Army, Navy, Air Force, sent down the coal mines or to work in a factory. However, one could avoid compulsory conscription by volunteering to serve in the service of one's choice before receiving the conscription notice.

Accordingly, I viewed the options open to me. I did not like the Army uniform and had heard tales of war in the trenches from World War 1. I decided against the Navy because I was not a particularly good swimmer, and in any case, I thought that wearing bell-bottom trousers on a freezing ship's deck would hamper my marriage prospects. Going down the mines would be claustrophobic, and working in a factory on lathes and machine tools would be soul destroying. I concluded that the RAF was for me, because they wore collars and ties, had a smart blue uniform, and after all, I might get to fly.

In April 1940, I attended an interview at an RAF recruiting office in Reading, volunteering to serve in the RAF and indicating a desire to train as a pilot. The interview went well, after which I was given a basic medical examination. Suddenly, I realised I was taking a large step into the unknown and was a little apprehensive about what the future might bring. In May I was told to report to Cardington in Bedfordshire for a full two-day aircrew medical. There I was given a more thorough examination covering every part of the anatomy, with particular attention to sight, hearing and physical fitness. This included being spun round in a chair and then being made to walk a straight line. I spent the night in a bell tent with other applicants, our feet all pointing to the tent-pole in the middle. I was then told to go home and await reporting instructions.

In the meantime, events had been unfolding abroad. The Germans had broken through Holland and Belgium and into France, followed by the BEF retreat from Dunkirk. The RAF had fought gallantly during the retreat but had lost 195 Hurricanes and seven squadrons of Fairey Battles in the process. Having consolidated their position on airfields in northern France, and assembled over 2,000 invasion barges in northern French ports, plus having 120 divisions of troops available, the German invasion of Britain (Operation Sea Lion) started with air raids over southern England, the Luftwaffe having some 2,669 aircraft at their disposal. So began the Battle of Britain, as it was later to become known. RAF Fighter Command were heavily outnumbered, with some 800 fighters, consisting mostly of Spitfires and Hurricanes plus a small collection of Defiants and Gladiators, but they were determined to stop the Germans at all costs.

In June, the Luftwaffe began bombing the principal RAF airfields in the south-east of England in addition to bombing southern coastal towns and convoys in the English Channel. The RAF had to revert to flying from makeshift airfields while every effort was made to repair their damaged bases. Despite this, the RAF inflicted heavy casualties on the Luftwaffe but in the process lost nearly 500 pilots and aircraft themselves. The Battle reached a crescendo in September, at which time the Germans realised they had not achieved the air superiority vital to the success of the invasion and were suffering unacceptable losses of aircraft and airmen. The RAF made many sacrifices, but they were so successful that the invasion was deferred, so that in September, the Germans resorted to the bombing of London.

I remember seeing the white contrails high in the sky and hearing the sound of machine guns over southern Britain as the battle was fought, and I firmly believe that the Battle of Britain was one of the most important in the history of this country – it certainly saved us from the Nazi jackboot. At the age of 18, I don't think the import of what was going on had really sunk in. Equally, the general public were looking on at the battle in the sky with a certain amount of detachment, except those actively involved directly beneath it all. The British propaganda machine was going full blast in ensuring that the British Bulldog would triumph over the Germans. There was some general public concern but a feeling that Britain would win in the end.

It was during the summer of 1940 that Winston Churchill said in one of his speeches, "The Navy can lose the war, but only the Air Force can win it. Therefore our supreme effort must be to gain overwhelming mastery in the air. The fighters are our salvation, but the bombers alone provide the means of victory."

It wasn't until late August that I got my call-up papers requiring me to report to Babbacombe near Torquay in Devon. My parents took me to Reading station and, clutching a small fibre suitcase, I travelled to Torquay, a little apprehensive about what awaited me. On arrival, a truck waited to convey me and other recruits to Babbacombe. We were billeted in a boarding-house that had been requisitioned. The furniture and carpets had been replaced with bare floorboards, the regulation iron bed, three 'biscuits' and a locker. The 'biscuits' were square mattresses filled with straw or something similar, which when laid in line formed a full mattress. Every morning these had to be stacked at the head of the bed, with sheets and blankets neatly folded on top for inspection, together with inspection of the locker.

Babbacombe
[courtesy of Torbay Library Services]

The next day we were marched to the stores located in Babbacombe Garage for the issue of our uniforms and clothing:

socks, two pairs, airman for the use of; underpants, two pairs, airman for the use of; and so on. We were given brown paper and string, so that having fitted into our uniforms, we could pack our civilian clothes, make them into a parcel, and take them to the stores to be sent to our homes. From that moment, we were in the RAF, and subject to military orders. To distinguish us as aircrew cadets, we wore a white flash tucked into the front of our service caps.

So service life began. We were marched to see the Medical Officer to be vaccinated and injected against typhus, typhoid and tetanus. The hypodermics were used over and over, time and time again, the needles being replaced only when they became blunt. Thereafter, we were taught to march to an area on which we practised our drills and marching, how to about-turn, line up, salute officers, and respond to orders. For the first time in my life, I was away from family and friends. Now I was among strangers in a strange environment and initially felt lonely. However, this soon vanished as the camaraderie of service life kicked in.

Babbacombe was a relatively small community at that time, with a number of hotels and boarding-houses fronted by a road, and between the road and the cliff-top was a large green area called The Downs on which we practised our marching and drills. On one such occasion, there were sudden shouts of "Down, down! Everyone down on the ground", just as a German Heinkel 111 bomber flew past 100 yards out to sea, level with the cliff-top, and firing its upper machine gun inland in our direction. By a miracle, no-one was hurt, but a number of windows were blown out of the boarding-houses and hotels in the background – our first introduction to enemy action.

At the end of two weeks, we were marched to Torquay station, and at midnight put in a railway coach attached to a London train. The train had to wait outside Bristol Temple Meads station while an air raid was in progress and then, after the 'All clear' was sounded, our coach was attached to a train heading into Wales. We waited outside Cardiff for another air-raid warning, and then the train slowly wended its way around the west coast of Wales. The comfort of our journey might have been improved if we had travelled in a corridor coach, and so, at many small stations en route there was a rush for the station toilets, with the little Welsh guard with his green flag and whistle knocking on station toilet doors shouting, "Come on, you boys, you are making my train late!" Finally, after 16 hours on the train, we arrived at Aberystwyth.

CHAPTER 3
Initial training

On arrival at Aberystwyth, we were marched to what had been the old Queen's Hotel, now converted to RAF use, with the inevitable iron beds, 'biscuit' mattresses, and lockers. From now on, the training programme was intense. Each morning started early, with PE on the seafront, so in plimsolls, shorts and singlets we were subjected to half an hour's exercises. The wind off Cardigan Bay was sometimes very cold at that time of the year, but the exercises kept us very fit.

Thereafter, we learned the theory of flight, aero engines and airframes, navigation, the phonetic alphabet, meteorology, stripping and reassembling machine guns, and learning to send Morse code at twelve words per minute with Aldis lamps and eighteen words per minute with the Morse key, plus enemy aircraft recognition. I enjoyed the navigation and map-reading exercises, and finding unfamiliar places in Britain using map co-ordinates, little knowing that a number of these places would become more familiar to me later on. There were question-and-answer sessions every morning and exams at the end of the week on Saturdays, plus a final exam at the end of the course. Failure to pass any exam meant being sent off the course and posted to some RAF ground job.

As at Babbacombe, on Sunday morning we had compulsory Church Parade, with personnel being marched off to the Church of England, Catholic, or Other Denominations (OD) churches. For a change, we sometimes attended each other's services. Sunday afternoons were free time. At the end of the course we were given a week's leave, and this meant travelling via Shrewsbury, Birmingham, Paddington, Waterloo and on to

Bentley in packed trains – a long journey in those wartime days. I was amazed when travelling on the Underground in London to see families settling down for the night on the platforms, to escape the nightly German air raids.

Queen's Hotel

Aberystwyth
[courtesy of Ceredigion Museum]

It was whilst on this leave that I married Audrey, a girl I had grown very fond of. I was still young, and fairly naïve, but there was a war on, and it was a time when no-one knew what would happen next, and indeed, if and when you might die. There was a feeling that one should live for today and grab what happiness one could. I was just nineteen, and Audrey only eighteen. At that time she was working in the Home Office in London, commuting daily and spending some of the time in air-raid shelters. Our honeymoon lasted one weekend.

Audrey and me

On returning to Aberystwyth, we were told that our next posting was not ready for us, so we were sent home for another five days' leave. I was then told to report to Ansty, a small grass airfield on the outskirts of Coventry. Here we were to be taught to fly Tiger Moths. These were sturdy and reliable aircraft, well able to withstand rough treatment, but they were not the easiest aircraft to control. We were now promoted to the exalted rank of Leading Aircraftsman (LAC), which meant that we were no longer the lowest form of life in the Air Force.

De Havilland Tiger Moth
[courtesy of Aeroplane *magazine]*

We arrived at the airfield in the afternoon, but spent the night in an air-raid shelter, because it so happened that this was 14th November 1940, the night that the Germans bombed Coventry for thirteen consecutive hours. The next morning we were loaded into lorries, complete with picks and shovels, to see what assistance we could give to the Civil Defence authorities. Our task was to help clear the roads into the city, search cellars to find trapped people and, where necessary, help extract the dead. The scene was chaotic. There was a smell from broken sewage pipes, escaping gas, smouldering ruins, plus a pervading smell of burnt flesh. People were wandering around in a daze; everything they possessed gone, all they had was what they stood up in.

About 600 people were killed in the raid, over 80 of whom were sheltering in the basement of the Owen Owen department store when it received a direct hit and was burnt out. To me, the whole scene was horrific and stomach turning, but we had a job to do, and by nightfall I was surprised at how hardened I had become to the terrible scenes. In searching cellars, we found no survivors but, incongruously, intact stocks of cigarettes and cigars under what had been a tobacconist, bottles of spirits and beer barrels under what had been a pub, and at ground level, a bank safe with the door blown ajar full of bank notes. However, we had important work to do and never considered the possibility of looting, which was just as well since the crime carried the death penalty, although I don't think that anyone was actually hanged, imprisonment with hard labour being the preferred penalty of the courts.

By the end of the day, help had come into Coventry from all the neighbouring cities, from Wolverhampton in the west to Nottingham in the east, and we were no longer needed. There is no doubt that the relentless sounds of the air raids that night and the subsequent appalling sights which I witnessed the next day in Coventry shaped and hardened my feelings against the enemy. As a result, I had no compunction about bombing Germany later in the war. As far as I was concerned, I was giving back the same treatment which they had dished out to the people of Coventry and the other towns and cities of Britain which were bombed.

LAST EDITION

This is the Gin Gordon's *Stands Supreme*

Midland D

No. 15,426. MIDLAND DAILY TELEGRAPH

Moonlight bombers attack from

BERLIN GETS B

Coventry bombed:
Casualties 1,000
Cathedral and shelters hit

"THE City of Coventry was heavily attacked last night," states a Ministry of Home Security communique issued this afternoon. "The scale of the raids was comparable with those of the largest night attacks on London."

"The enemy were heavily engaged by intensive A.A. fire which kept them at a great height and hindered accurate bombing of industrial targets, but the City itself suffered very seriously."

"PRELIMINARY REPORTS INDICATE THAT THE NUMBER OF CASUALTIES MAY BE IN THE NEIGHBOURHOOD OF A THOUSAND.

"The attack was begun by the scattering of incendiary bombs over a wide area. Fires broke out at many points indiscriminate bombardment of the whole city owed.

"It is feared that extensive damage was done and many buildings destroyed, including the cathedral.

"THE PEOPLE OF COVENTRY BORE THEIR ORDEAL WITH GREAT COURAGE.

"It is known that at least two enemy aircraft were shot down during the attack."

Many fires were caused, and considerable damage was done.

Full reports are not yet available, but it is feared that casualties are heavy.

"In attacks on other towns in the Midlands shops and houses were damaged but although some people were killed or injured, the number of casualties was not large.

"In the London area bombs were dropped by intermittent raiders. Houses and some other buildings were destroyed. Some people were killed and some injured.

"Bombs were also dropped in a number of widely separated districts of England and in North Wales. In a few of these houses were also damaged but the number of casualties was very small."

London raid

The largest number of raiders ever to cross the East Coast at night came over in waves, and several bombs were dropped in a town on the S.E. Coast.

The London "alert" came nearly an hour later than on Wednesday. During a short period when heavy gunfire was heard, bombs crashed down on

"CITY OF THREE SPIRES"

Coutesy

'Coventry pays for Munich'
—Nazi radio

A CLAIM that the German Air Force last night "struck a violent blow in return for the abortive British raid on the Party Celebration in Munich," was broadcast to-day by the German radio.

Apart from London, and other targets of military importance," the announcer stated, "Coventry—the centre of the British aircraft industry—was raided by waves of strong forces of German bombers.

"Early in the evening bombs of the heaviest calibres were dropped on numerous aircraft engine works and aircraft accessories' plants.

"At 5 p.m. more than 20 large fires lit the way for the following bombing squadrons which continued their attacks throughout the night.

"The defences were helpless against the vigorous attack of the Luftwaffe.

"The increasing fires caused big explosions, indicating that not only factories but also large stocks of raw materials, some manufactured goods, and finishing products had been destroyed."

ITALIA

Midland Daily Telegraph Saturday 16th November 1940

MIDLAND DAILY TELEGRAPH, Saturday, 16 November,

"Their Wounds are Sacred"

WARSAW and London and so many other cities, Polish and English, large and small, have already covered themselves in immortal glory.

Their wounds: their ruins, their shattered works of art, historical buildings and monuments, will remain for ever sacred symbols of heroism, patriotism, and the highest spirit of sacrifice.

"The only way to that better future leads through the complete and final victory of Great Britain" — M. Paderewski yesterday.

And This Was The Ordeal of Coventry

"THE PEOPLE BORE IT WITH GREAT COURAGE"

Bad As London's Worst

THE City of Coventry was heavily attacked last night, states Ministry of Home Security communique issued yesterday afternoon. "The scale of the raids was comparable with those of the long night attacks on London.

Midland Daily Telegraph Saturday 16th November 1940

The next morning our pilot training began in earnest. We were issued with a Sidcot Flying Suit (a type of coverall), flying helmet and goggles.

Johnnie Trotman and Tiger Moths

My instructor was tall in stature but short on temper. We started with familiarisation of the aircraft on the ground and understanding of the control system. Then, in the air, I learned that if you pushed the stick forward the nose of the plane went down and, conversely, if you pulled the stick back the nose of the aircraft came up. The trouble came when I had to learn to turn the plane left or right. This required making a Rate 1 turn (30 degrees), which I found very difficult to do precisely.

I had only ever flown once before, on a five-shilling trip with Alan Cobham's Flying Circus, so was very nervous, and it was very cold in an open cockpit. Needless to say, when I tried the turn, the plane either gained or lost height, or I increased or decreased the rate of turn. After three unsuccessful attempts, my instructor was shouting at me, and after two further unsuccessful attempts, he snatched the controls out of my hands, threw the plane all over the sky, then shouted, "Right, let's try it again."

After this rather brutal treatment, my enthusiasm and confidence started to wane, and I began to think I should transfer to a ground job, though this would have been a great disappointment. However, after seven hours' flying, I was suddenly transferred to a Sgt Barraclough for assessment and further training. Sgt Barraclough was a plump, jolly Yorkshire man of infinite patience, who had been a civilian flying instructor before the war. Under his tuition, encouragement and praise, my enthusiasm and confidence returned, and he made me keen to succeed.

Then came the day when, after completing two circuits of the field, my instructor got out of his cockpit and said, "Now it's all yours. Make your solo a good one; good luck." It was a tremendous thrill and a great responsibility to go solo for the first time. Flying alone without an instructor present was both frightening and awe-inspiring. The day was perfect, with bright sunshine, and my circuit went extremely well. The landing was a perfect 'three pointer' (all three wheels touched the ground together). Now thoroughly exhilarated with my achievement, I taxied over to the control tower and switched off. Sgt Barraclough congratulated me on my success. I noticed that a crowd of civilians had been watching the flying and asked him who they were. It was revealed that they were members of the national press, who, having seen the progress being made in repairing Coventry after the air raid, had come to Ansty to report on the young RAF airmen who were trained to fight back against the Germans. As a result, my first solo flight was mentioned in the *News Chronicle* the next day.

That night, along with three other lads, one of whom had also soloed at the same time as me, I made my way to the local village pub to celebrate our success. I have to say that at that point in my life I was teetotal. My mother was completely teetotal, although she did excel herself on Christmas Day when she would make an exception and drink a ginger beer. My father drank the odd pint from time to time, and to celebrate my joining the RAF he had bought me a pint of local brewery ale in our local pub. This tasted foul, and put me off drinking alcohol from then on.

In the pub at Ansty, the publican had run out of brewery beer, and, like many of his colleagues in wartime, had resorted to brewing his own beer. A pint was thrust into my hand, and on tasting it, I found it to be rather sweet and quite tasty. However, after drinking half a glass, I found that when I spoke my lips didn't seem to coincide with the words I was saying; I was getting tiddly. At this point, we four lads were challenged to a game of darts 501-up by some of the locals. Our team started the play, but by the time it was my turn to throw, we were losing. I squinted at the dart board, which somehow seemed a long way away and asked what I should aim for. They said, "Treble top." I aimed the dart in the general direction of the board and hit treble top! I repeated the action with a double top and finally clinched the match with an appropriate double. There was uproar! Our team cheered, and the locals accused me of being a professional darts player. Nevertheless, another drink was thrust into my hand and the rest of the evening passed in a haze. Needless to say, the next morning I had a thick head, but I had achieved a double success; I had gone solo and won a darts match all in one day.

So flying continued, practising all the necessary aspects of controlling aircraft, including instrument flying, formation flying, map reading, cross-country flying, and navigation exercises. Instrument flying was practised both in the air and on the ground in the Link Trainer, an early type of flight simulator, which was highly sensitive and, in our minds, a form of torture chamber. It was necessary to carry out a specified number of hours on the Link Trainer over the period of the course.

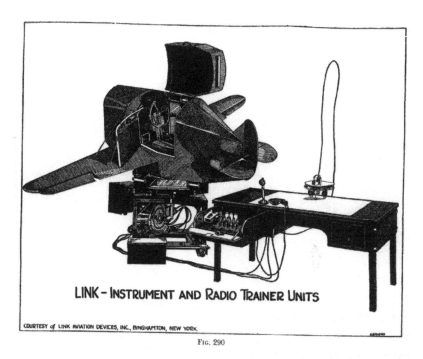

LINK – INSTRUMENT AND RADIO TRAINER UNITS

FIG. 290

FIG. 290. The Link unit consists of a dummy airplane, complete with wings and control surfaces, and an instructor's table equipped with radio, telephone, and a charting device that keeps an accurate record of your "flight." The dummy plane is mounted on a turntable, and this, in turn, is mounted on a stationary base.

Don't make the mistake of thinking that this "dummy" plane is easy to manage. It pitches, rolls, turns, simulates dives and climbs, and can spin so rapidly that you will get the same sensations of vertigo that you would in the overcast. Bumps can be turned on to give you all the practice you need in rough air. In fact, the trainer is far less stable and much more sensitive to control than a regular plane, for the simple reason that you can get much

314

Link Trainer equipment

41

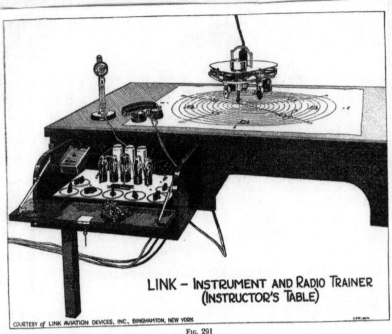

LINK – INSTRUMENT AND RADIO TRAINER (INSTRUCTOR'S TABLE)

Fig. 291

better training in a hypersensitive plane than you can in a slower and more stable machine.

The training unit is connected both by radio and by phone to the instructor's table. Over the telephone he gives you various commands and instructions; over the radio come radio-beam signals to give you thorough experience in flying the airways while you are still safe on the ground.

Your training begins with the simplest of operations—making constant-rate turns to the right and left. You make these turns first with the hood up, later with the hood down. An important part of your training at this stage is learning to make accurately timed turns without the aid of a clock by *counting* the required number of seconds.

Link Trainer equipment

Our initial navigation cross-country flight was to fly from Coventry, to Rugby, then to Nuneaton and back to Coventry. This was not a problem, because the main railway line from Birmingham to London ran through Coventry to Rugby, the main railway line from London to the north-west ran through Rugby to Nuneaton, and in those days, a railway line ran from

Nuneaton to Coventry. Therefore, so long as one knew the points of the compass and followed the railway lines, the cross-country would present no problem.

On our course, we had a chap whom we nicknamed 'Mad Jack'. He was desperate to qualify as a fully fledged pilot so that he could go on to fly Spitfires. Jack set off on his initial cross-country and flew from Coventry to Rugby. Turning on course towards Nuneaton, he spotted a train pulling out of Rugby heading towards the north-west. I must mention at this point that the railway line on this section has a canal running alongside it for some miles, and halfway to Nuneaton the line and the canal pass through a cutting in a hill where a high bridge passes over both the line and the canal with separate arches, one for the railway and one for the canal.

Without any ado, and regardless of his limited training, Mad Jack dived down and flew along just above the canal and alongside the train, waving nonchalantly to the passengers. They presumably thought he must have been one of those wonderful pilots they had heard so much about in the Battle of Britain. Jack was so busy concentrating on holding his position and showing off that when he glanced ahead, he realised to his horror that he had flown into the cutting and, what was more, the bridge was towering over him. He had only one choice, he had to fly through the arch of the bridge over the canal, and this is what he did. The passengers in the train were wild with excitement at this daring pilot's exploits, and waved furiously. Inside the cockpit, Jack's arms and legs were shaking and his heart was pumping furiously as he quickly climbed back up to his correct height, continued his cross-country, and landed back at Ansty.

Jack later told us in confidence what had happened, and asked us to swear not to tell the instructors, for fear he would be grounded permanently. The following weekend, several of us cycled with Jack out to the bridge and, after measuring its span, and knowing the wing span of the Tiger Moth, we were able to establish that Jack had cleared the bridge with barely six inches to spare on either side.

One windy day, I climbed into a Tiger Moth with the ground crew holding and steadying the wings. I opened the throttle fully, and, because of the high wind, the aircraft left the ground almost immediately. On closing the throttle to normal cruising speed, I found to my surprise that I was actually flying backwards relative to the ground. When it came time to land again, it was necessary to open the throttle wide and point the aircraft towards the ground. On my arrival, the ground crew had to seize the wings and anchor the aircraft to the ground.

Because Coventry was still in the throes of recovery, three colleagues and I set off one Saturday night in a car that belonged to one of them to visit a cinema in nearby Leicester. We parked the car in a side street adjacent to the cinema and went in to enjoy the film. During the performance, the manager notified the audience that an air raid was in progress: those people wishing to proceed to the air-raid shelter were given directions, but in the meantime the film show would continue for those who wished to remain in the cinema. With great bravado, we stayed until the end of the film, left the cinema, turned the corner to where the car was parked, and saw to our horror that less than 100 yards from the car, firemen were desperately trying to quench a huge blaze in a four-storey factory. Flames roared above and up the front of the building, with masonry falling into the street. The chap who owned the car ran like a hare, unlocked his car, reversed at high speed, did a rapid three-point turn, whereon we all jumped in and departed the scene quickly. Fortunately, the car was untouched by the heat or falling masonry.

Towards the end of the course we were taught aerobatics. I could happily manage stall turns, spins and loops, but could not seem to co-ordinate stick and rudder to successfully complete rolls, half rolls and rolls off the top. I hated sitting in the open cockpit when the plane was on its back, suspended by the harness, looking up at the ground. Consequently, it was recommended that I should be put forward for twin-engine aircraft training, to which I was happy to agree. Accordingly, I was posted to No.3 Service Flying Training School at South Cerney. It was February 1941.

CHAPTER 4
No.3 Service Flying Training School, South Cerney, Gloucestershire

South Cerney was a pre-war RAF station, well equipped and well established. At this time, Audrey decided she wished to accompany me on this posting, so on the first weekend there I obtained lodgings in Cirencester, and the following weekend dashed home to Bentley, picked up Audrey and together we took the 90-mile journey to Cirencester in an elderly Austin 7 with fabric body and wire wheels, an oversized perambulator. I had obtained a living-out allowance from the RAF, and thereafter commuted into the camp either by car when the meagre petrol allowance allowed, or on bicycle or bus. From now on, instead of living in the camp and being subject to disciplined living conditions, I was enjoying the relative comforts of domestic bliss.

The aircraft at South Cerney were Airspeed Oxfords, a fairly docile twin-engine aircraft with retractable undercarriage and flaps but with fixed-pitch propellers. With two people on board, it would safely climb on one engine. It was based on the Airspeed Envoy first flown in 1934, was of wooden construction with stressed skin wings, and an ideal training aircraft.

Airspeed Oxford
[courtesy bing.com images]

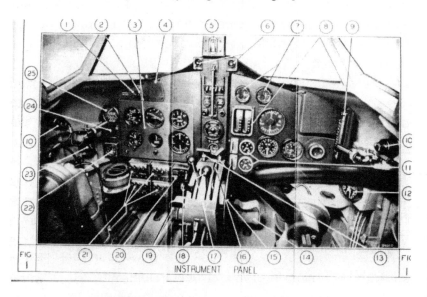

Airspeed Oxford instrument panel
[courtesy Crecy Publishing Ltd, Manchester]

My instructor was a Sgt Sly, far removed in personality from his name, and good at his job. Progress was rapid in all aspects of training, covering handling on the ground and in the air, single-engine flying, instrument and formation flying, cross-countries, and night flying. I flew my first solo flight in the Oxford after three hours and fifty minutes of tuition.

After completing the mandatory basic day cross-country with an instructor, and carrying out the same cross-country on our own, we were allowed to decide the route of the next cross-country of our own, subject, of course, to approval. I chose a route Cirencester – Reading – Northampton – Cirencester, and this was approved as a flight plan. Accordingly, I set off, and once out of sight of South Cerney, opened the throttles and increased the speed of the aircraft.

At Reading, instead of turning left for Northampton, I turned right, and flew the 15 miles to my home village of Bentley, map reading as I went, although I had unofficially worked out the course in advance, where, with great daring, excitement, and not a lot of experience, I circled my home at low level. My parents ran into the road and waved, assuming it was me flying the plane. I flew down the main road in the village, looking back and waving cheerily, then turned to look forward, whereupon I immediately pulled hard back on the control column, climbing steeply, in time for the propeller tips to pass through the top twigs of a row of poplar trees adjacent to the vicarage. It was a close shave and a great shock. My heart was in my mouth. If I had turned to look forward two seconds later, I would have crashed into the trees and been killed. I then remembered the warnings we had been given about carrying out such dangerous manoeuvres, particularly when trying to show off in front of relatives and friends. With my heart thumping, I flew back to Reading and continued on to Northampton at high speed, then continued back for Cirencester. I arrived back on Estimated

Time of Arrival (ETA), having improperly altered my ETAs at Reading and Northampton to disguise my little detour.

Because South Cerney was a busy airfield, some use was made of Kemble, a neighbouring maintenance airfield, and Bibury, a small grass field adjacent to a village to the east of South Cerney. Night flying at South Cerney was not a problem, because as a pre-war airfield it was suitably equipped. Bibury, on the other hand, had to make do with rudimentary equipment, and the grass runway lighting for night-flying landings consisted of 'goose-neck' flares. These were like old-fashioned oil-cans with a long narrow spout, but very much larger, filled with a mixture of kerosene and petrol and with a wick stuck up the spout which was then lit. Six goose flares were set in a line with one offset at the windward end to make a half 'T'. It was quite difficult at first to achieve satisfactory landings, particularly as we were not allowed to use landing lights, relying only on normal navigation lights for flying and negotiating our way round the field, in complete darkness. After two hours' instruction, I was sent to practise on my own.

One night I took over an aircraft from another pupil at about 11pm to practise take-off and landings. After three-quarters of an hour, I suddenly received a call over the radio that an air-raid warning was in force. This meant that there was a German night fighter intruder in the area. At that moment, I was on the downwind leg of the circuit, preparing to lower the undercarriage prior to landing, so, in accordance with instructions, I switched off my navigation lights and turned the cockpit lighting right down. In the meantime, the goose-neck flare path below had been extinguished, so that I was left flying in the dark, having to use my own initiative.

I decided to fly a square circuit pattern using compass and watch, but this was difficult because the watch I was wearing was a gift given to me by my parents when I joined up. The watch had only hour and minute hands and was very difficult to see in the very subdued light in the cockpit. Half an hour passed by and I could feel the goose pimples down the back of my neck. I knew that out there, sharing the pitch dark of the sky, was a German night fighter intruder looking for me and ready to shoot me down, as had happened previously at another airfield, when two aircraft practising night flying had been shot down, killing both pilots. And to make matters worse, by now I was running short of fuel. The policy was that if one was likely to run out of fuel in these circumstances one had to climb up to 5,000 feet, switch off everything in the plane and bail out by parachute, which did not present itself to me as an agreeable prospect.

At last, after three-quarters of an hour, the all-clear signal was given, much to my relief. When all the lights came on below, I found, having allowed for the wind, I was halfway between South Cerney and Bibury. Without further ado, I headed for South Cerney and landed with very little fuel left in the tanks – and a feeling of great relief!

So the course continued to its conclusion, and after a satisfactory test with the Chief Flying Instructor, when surprisingly I was rated as an above-average pilot, I was presented, along with all my course colleagues, with my Wings at an appropriate ceremony – a very proud moment! We were now qualified pilots. Additionally, we were now promoted from Leading Aircraftmen to Sergeants, with appropriate benefits and increased pay. Everyone was posted to Operational Training Units except for me. Surprisingly, I was posted to No.2 Central Flying School to train as an instructor.

CHAPTER 5
No.2 Central Flying School, Cranwell

RAF Cranwell was commissioned on 1st April 1916 as the training establishment for the Royal Naval Air Service. Two years later to the day it passed to the Royal Air Force, and on 5th February 1920 it became the first Military Air Academy in the world under the command of Air Commodore CAH Longcroft. It is said that the site for Cranwell was chosen by sending a young RNAS pilot to fly around Lincolnshire until he saw a suitable site which was large enough and flat enough for a training airfield. He must have been spoilt for choice because Lincolnshire is not known as Bomber County for nothing; during the war, aerodromes were located every few miles across the county, and even today it has more operational airfields than any other county in Britain. Originally a collection of wooden huts built in the Lincolnshire countryside, the present stone buildings in the style of Sir Christopher Wren were completed in September 1933 at a cost of £321,000.

In May 1941 I reported to Cranwell, considered to be 'the Sandhurst of the RAF'. However, because of the war, most of the highly disciplined procedures adopted in peacetime had been dropped in favour of all energies being directed to turning out pilots and instructors, and testing aircraft. Audrey came with me, and we lived out in Sleaford from where I commuted daily. Training commenced immediately, with three weeks spent learning to instruct in Avro Tutor biplanes, followed by three weeks learning to instruct in Airspeed Oxfords. We were issued with an instructor's handbook with appropriate wording covering every part of the 28-chapter syllabus which we had to learn by heart.

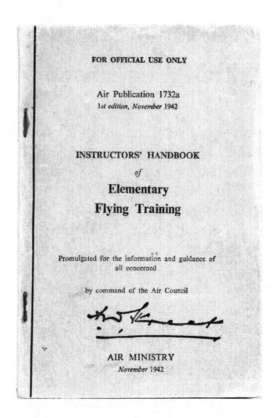

Instructors Handbook, November 1942

The Avro Tutor
[courtesy of Aeroplane *magazine]*

The Tutor was a fairly old aircraft, but robustly built, easily suited to training, and easy to fly. The teaching followed a strict pattern. We were given a session in the classroom relative to a particular subject of training, followed by a short session in the air with an instructor. Thereafter two pupils went up in an aircraft together and practised the subject. This pattern was repeated until the entire syllabus was covered – needless to say, we were flying seven days a week.

The syllabus covered -

1 Familiarity with cockpit layout

2 Preparation for flight

3 Air experience

4 Effect of controls

5 Taxiing

6 Straight and level flight

7 Climbing

8 Descending

9 Stalling

10 Medium turns

11 Gliding and climbing turns

12 Taking off into wind

13 Approach and landing

14 Spinning

15 First solo

16 Side-slipping

17 Steep turns

18 Instrument flying

19 Low flying

20 Taking off and landing out of wind

21 Precautionary landings

22 Forced landings

23 Action in the event of fire

24 Restarting engine in flight

25 Aerobatics

26 Night flying

27 Pilot navigation

28 Formation flying

One day, P/O Johnson, naturally called 'Johnnie', and I were sent up together to practise 'Action to be taken in the event of an engine failure'. This entailed climbing to 3,000 feet, throttling back the engine to simulate engine failure, putting the plane into a glide, checking to find the cause of the engine failure, finding a grass field in which to make an emergency landing, and making a practice approach on the field without actually landing.

It was my turn first to carry out the exercise, and talking through the necessary instructional 'patter', I brought the plane down to about 30 feet on an approach to a field situated in the local low-flying area, then opened the throttle and climbed the plane back up to 3,000 feet while Johnnie reviewed my performance. Johnnie then took over control of the plane and went through his practice performance and 'patter'. He chose another field and brought the plane down to about 30 feet, but when he opened the throttle, the engine stalled and wouldn't respond. We quickly decided he should land the plane in the field, we would find out why the engine had not responded, repair it if we could, and fly out again. Johnnie put the plane down on the ground, applied the brakes, and it looked as if we would stop just short of a twelve-foot-high thick thorn hedge. Suddenly, there was a tremendous roar as the engine kicked into full throttle. Throwing us back in our cockpits, the plane rocketed forward straight through the thorn hedge, leaving the wings and the undercarriage behind and the wooden propeller shattered. Still careering forwards, the engine screeched like a banshee until it finally stopped twenty feet into the neighbouring potato field, leaving us marooned in the upright fuselage.

We sat stunned for a moment, suffering from whiplash and my nose bleeding from striking the padded front of the cockpit. Then, still sitting in the fuselage, we decided that, instead of opening the throttle gently at 30 feet, Johnnie had slammed it open, flooding the carburettor. The engine had stalled, but the propeller was still windmilling and sucking air and petrol through the carburettor. Concentrating on his landing, Johnnie had forgotten to close the throttle. At this point, the engine had decided to open up fully, with disastrous results. We then had a discussion about how we were going to tell the instructors and the Commanding Officer back at Cranwell that we had just wrecked one of the aircraft. Then we climbed out of the cockpits, our limbs trembling, and went for help. As a result of this, Johnnie got an endorsement in his Log Book, but was allowed to continue training.

In the third week, we had to learn to teach aerobatics in the Tutor. I realised my limitations in this area, but struggled on. I performed satisfactorily with stall turns, spins and loops, but came up against the same problem I had encountered in Elementary Flying Training School (EFTS) Ansty. I lacked sufficient co-ordination with stick and rudder in performing rolls, half rolls and rolls off the top.

It was at about this time on the course that we were suddenly confined to quarters. All of a sudden, we heard a strange whining noise, and, rushing to the windows, saw a small aeroplane take off and climb steeply − it had no propeller! What we had witnessed was the Gloster Jet E28/39 prototype aircraft on test, with the revolutionary engine designed by Frank Whittle. With a machine like that, we thought, we must surely win the war. We badly needed some stimulus at that time in 1941, when things were proving very difficult for Britain, although we felt some relief from the pressure of possible invasion when Germany decided to attack Russia.

The last three weeks of the course were spent learning to instruct on Airspeed Oxfords, and I felt much more confident and competent with this machine. On completion of the course, I was posted to RAF Shawbury.

Gloster Jet E28/39

CHAPTER 6
No.11 Service Flying Training School, Shawbury

When I was posted to No.11 SFTS at Shawbury as an instructor on Airspeed Oxfords, Audrey came with me and we lived out in Shrewsbury. Pupils came to Shawbury having completed their Initial Flying Training on Tiger Moths, and it was our job to convert them to be able to fly twin-engine aircraft. In the process I gained confidence and authority.

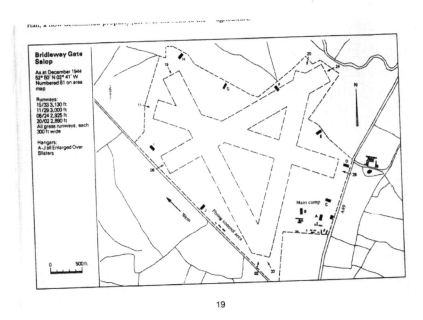

19

Bridleway Gate
[courtesy Langrist Caiger Publishers]

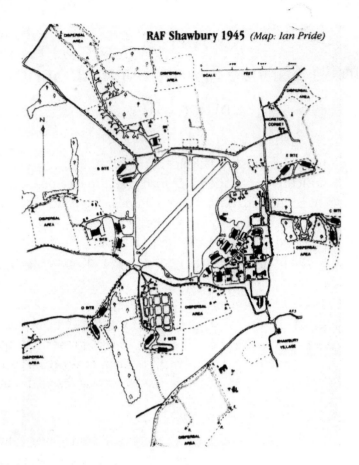

RAF Shawbury 1945 *(Map: Ian Pride)*

RAF Shawbury
[courtesy of Langrist Caiger Publishers]

The Airspeed Oxford was a relatively easy aircraft to handle, but on the early models it had one problem in that the undercarriage lever and the flap lever were side by side on the central binnacle and were almost indistinguishable from one another. One had to be very careful to choose the right lever, particularly when carrying out aborted landings or 'overshoots' near the ground. These were when, having made an approach to land at the airfield, a pilot changed his mind for whatever reason, abandoned the approach, opened the throttles and climbed away from the runway to try to land again. If the flap lever was selected in error instead of the undercarriage lever when flying close to the ground, the aircraft would sink like a free-falling lift and strike the ground with disastrous results.

On one occasion when teaching a pupil 'overshoots', he pulled up the flap lever in error. However, being very alert to this problem, I brought my fist down onto his hand hard, thereby forcing the lever back into its normal position. He shouted in protest, but, as I explained to him, I was rather keen to go on living. A week later, a pupil flying on his own pulled up the flap lever in error, causing the aircraft to crash and killing the pilot.

There were quite a few fatalities during training and, like other instructors, I was living on my nerves when pupils were being taught to land, take off, and stall in the air. There was no margin for error. Night-flying training continued at Shawbury where the facilities were adequate, but it presented some nerve-racking moments with some pupils. In order to cope with the number of courses, some night flying was carried out at Cranage.

In the July of 1941, Audrey returned to the south, went into a nursing home in Chawton near Alton and, after a difficult time, gave birth to our daughter. Soon afterwards she returned to Shrewsbury with the baby, and back to our digs. It was wonderful to be a father and I was very proud of my daughter, whom we named Sonia, although I couldn't help but worry about the world that we had brought her into, with the tide of the war very definitely flowing against us. The year had started with the defeat of the Italians in the Western Desert, but shortly afterwards, General Rommel entered the desert campaign with crack German troops and our 8th Army was struggling to keep him from seizing the Suez Canal. At home, our towns and cities were being bombed nightly, causing death and destruction to the civilian population, and in May, Crete was lost to the Germans, despite heroic fighting. However, that month did bring one ray of hope with the sinking of the German battleship *Bismarck*; even so, the U-boats were winning the Battle of the Atlantic. Some sense of relief came at last in June when the Germans invaded Russia, though we felt sorry for the Russians. Finally, in December came the news that the Japanese had attacked Pearl Harbor, at long last bringing the United States into the war.

By this time, the RAF had a total of 500 bombers, although only 230 were available for night-flying operations. German targets were being bombed, but with adverse weather conditions and inadequate navigational aids, results were unsatisfactory. Desperate efforts were being made to improve this situation. By 1942, the job I was doing began to lose its shine. As each new course arrived, one went through the training programme again and again, and I had a yearning to move on to an operational bomber squadron. This came about in an unexpected manner and gives truth to the saying that you should be careful what you wish for.

One of the training sessions we had to give was to teach pilots to fly very low to prevent enemy fighters from getting underneath the aircraft where they were most vulnerable. One day I took a pupil to the designated low-flying area near Wheaton Aston just north of the A5, and as he was reluctant to fly low, I decided to give him a demonstration. Flying a twin-engine aircraft at about 120 miles per hour just above the ground was a thrilling, exciting, and dangerous exercise, but it certainly got the adrenalin going. Initially, my pupil seemed quite alarmed and concerned at my demonstration, but then the thrill and excitement of what we were doing got the better of him and he began to enjoy it. I took the aircraft down as low as I could, hopping over hedges, flying between trees, avoiding power lines and a variety of other obstructions. Suddenly, as we flashed over a hedgerow, we came across an aerodrome under construction.

The runways were laid out, but the rest of the area was a sea of mud. A 4-wheel site caravan had been placed in the middle of the construction area and was now directly in my flight path. As we hurtled towards it at barely twenty feet, with the ground passing beneath us in a blur, I saw two men standing on the veranda of the caravan viewing the progress of the site work. Without any change of course or height, I continued to bear down upon the little structure until, at the last moment, I gave the nose of the Oxford the merest lift and roared over the caravan with scarcely more than ten feet to spare, rattling and shaking it with the backwash from the propellers. As I carried on with my demonstration, I was vaguely aware that the two men, seeing an aircraft flying straight towards them at the level of the caravan, and clearly fearing for their lives, had desperately dived off the veranda and straight into the mud!

The next morning I was called into the Wing Commander's office and given a severe dressing-down. It appeared that the two men who had dived into the mud the previous day were the site surveyor and the Group Captain, the Officer Commanding RAF Shawbury. The Wing Commander left me in no doubt that the Group Captain was enraged at my low-flying antics, was extremely upset at getting his nice clean uniform dirty and especially by the fact that his hat, complete with 'scrambled eggs', had flown off and been blown about in the mud, requiring specialist cleaning. My Flying Log Book was endorsed, 'As a Flying Instructor – below average'. My days as an instructor were over for the time being. I was posted forthwith to No.23 Operational Training Unit at Pershore in Worcestershire. Taken altogether, I was rather pleased with the whole episode as I was keen to get to an OTU and thence onto operations and was not at all bothered about the endorsement or the fate of the Group Captain.

CHAPTER 7
No.23 Operational Training Unit, Pershore Worcestershire

Pershore OTU was a unit where pilots, navigators, wireless operators, bomb aimers and gunners who had been trained at their various schools were brought together to form aircrews. The aircraft at Pershore were Wellington Mk Ics with Bristol Pegasus engines, and had been retired from operational use, though they were still reliable and airworthy. The Wellington was an immensely strong aircraft with its criss-cross 'geodetic' construction designed by the remarkable scientist Barnes Wallis, whose inventions included the 'bouncing bomb' later used with great success in the famous Dambuster raids.

This larger aircraft was a challenge to fly, compared with those I had flown hitherto and I looked forward to being able to handle what seemed a much more formidable aeroplane. After just over two hours' instruction, I went solo, and found the Wellington a good machine to fly.

File: WellingtonBomber.jpg
From Wikipedia, the free encyclopedia

Vickers Wellington bomber
[courtesy Wikipedia]

Vickers Wellington instrument panel
[courtesy of Crecy Publishing Ltd, Manchester]

Once again, Audrey came along with Sonia, and we lived out in Pershore in digs with a very nice and homely couple.

At Pershore, I was crewed up with three Australians and an Englishman. The Australians looked at me and said irreverently, "Christ, our pilot is a bloody Pom!" My reply was, "Christ, my crew are bloody Australian colonials", which was an appropriate slight upon them since Australia is most definitely not a colony. Having thus insulted each other, we got down to working together and formed a very fine team. They were Jim Sedger, Harry Mayne, Reg Moncton and my fellow Englishman, Andrew Pike. We flew daylight navigation cross-countries and practised dropping small 10lb bombs on the bombing ranges. This was followed by night cross-countries and night bombing practice.

Two-thirds of the way through the course, Air Chief Marshall Arthur Harris decided that, for the purposes of morale and prestige, the RAF should carry out its first 1,000 Bomber raid. Harris did not have anywhere near 1,000 aircraft at his disposal in Bomber Command, so had to borrow from Coastal Command and Training Command to make up the numbers. The aircraft from Training Command Operational Training Units were crewed by trainees but supervised by an experienced operational instructor. Four aircraft went from Pershore and my crew and I were one of the crews chosen to help make up the numbers. However, because of my instructional experience and having flown nearly 500 hours, there was no need for us to be supervised.

In the morning we checked our aircraft, ensuring all equipment was working, then handed the aeroplane over to the ground crew to fuel and load the bombs, a mixture of 500lb bombs and incendiaries. We attended a highly secret briefing, picked up our flying equipment and boarded our retired Wellington. There was nervous anticipation throughout the aircraft; this was our first operational trip! We had to acquit ourselves well. We flew across the Midlands, East Anglia, the North Sea, Holland and on to Cologne. At the Dutch coast we encountered our first experience of German flak [anti-aircraft fire], but by using evasion tactics of weaving the aircraft and varying our height, we were not hit. After that came our concern about being attacked by German night fighters, but despite keeping a sharp lookout, we did not see any.

At Cologne there was a bright moon and the visibility was excellent; we were able to bomb our target quite accurately. It was amazing to see the bridges over the Rhine and Cologne Cathedral rising virtually unscathed in the middle of the fires in the city. This reminded me of the picture of St Paul's Cathedral standing out against the flames of the London Blitz. That photograph had been taken by the *Daily Mail*'s chief photographer, Herbert Mason, from the roof of the *Mail* offices on the night of 29th December 1940 and had appeared on the paper's front page two days later; it was a picture which was to become the iconic image of the Blitz for so many people.

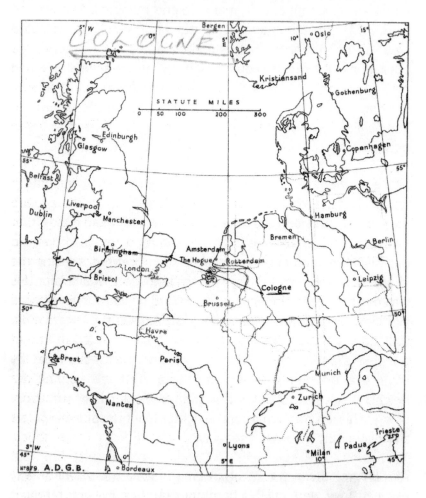

Route to Cologne

Harris had decided that all 1,047 aircraft taking part in this operation should take the same route and fly at the same speed but at different altitudes to avoid collision. This was the first time that Bomber Command had used the bomber stream tactic, and in the space of just ninety minutes, the entire stream had bombed the city and was on its way home. There was no doubt that the huge volume of aircraft used in the raid had overwhelmed the defences around the city. We returned to Pershore, relieved to know our first operation was over and we had not experienced the amount of flak we had expected nor seen any German night fighters. Once on the ground, the tension we had all felt was now gone. We attended a debriefing by the Station Intelligence Officer, and then, after consuming the traditional 'flying breakfast' of bacon and eggs given to operational aircrews on their return from a night raid and a special treat in those times of rationing, fell into bed.

Two nights later we were sent to bomb Essen in the Ruhr, in the second of the 1,000 Bomber raids. On this occasion, the Station Commander decided to fly with us. He was an old-timer who had flown in the First World War, and he was happy to keep providing us with coffee from a flask together with the chocolate he had obtained from some source or another. He was determined to be with us on this flight, though I doubted whether he had been officially authorised to do so, and we did wonder why he had chosen to come with us instead of one of the other crews from Pershore. In any event, as a crew we were happy to have him and his chocolate with us and counted it a privilege. Unfortunately, the weather over Essen was very cloudy, and it was impossible to accurately pinpoint the target so we had to bomb on 'dead reckoning' through the clouds. This time we encountered heavy anti-aircraft fire but fortunately were not hit, and neither did we see any enemy night fighters that troubled us. Andrew Pike, my rear gunner, did see an Me110 shot down, although this was difficult to authenticate with the Intelligence Officer at our de-brief afterwards. We returned to base satisfied that we had done the best we could under the circumstances. Two operations down – twenty-eight to go!

The following day we were told that there was no further reason to continue our training as we were already operational. Accordingly, we were sent on leave prior to a posting to an operational Bomber Command squadron.

CHAPTER 8
The start of operations first tour

A t this point, having had experience of flying over Germany, I realised that there were considerable dangers in being posted to an active squadron and the distinct possibility of being injured, killed or shot down over hostile territory and taken prisoner.

I therefore decided it would be foolish to have Audrey and baby Sonia accompany me. If anything should happen to me, she would be in the difficult position of having to pack up clothing, personal effects, pushchair and baby and travelling probably from Yorkshire to Kings Cross, in slow, packed trains, cross London to Waterloo and then on to her parents in Farnham, on her own. She didn't like the idea, but accepted the logic of the argument. It was June 1942.

My crew and I were first posted to RAF Binbrook in Lincolnshire. The aircraft in use there were Wellington Mark 2s equipped with Rolls Royce Merlin engines. It was known that these engines were prone to glycol leaks, accounting for some losses. We were therefore very pleased to be told that our posting to Binbrook was an error, and that we were to move on to a Royal Australian Air Force squadron, No.460 based at RAF Breighton in south Yorkshire, just north of the River Humber, near Hull.

We duly reported to Breighton, but the CO was away on leave so we could not be interviewed right away. We therefore reported to the flight office, and in due course carried out familiarisation flights in the area in the Wellington Mark IV with which the squadron was equipped. This aircraft was fitted with

American Pratt and Whitney twin Wasp engines, and, as their name implied, they were excessively noisy, particularly when taking off, causing much rattling of the eardrums. After nearly a week, the Wing Commander returned from leave and we were called to his office for interview. We lined up in front of his desk and he pointed to me as the pilot, saying in a strong Australian accent, "Right, what's your name and where are you from?" When I told him, he gave me a hard look and said loudly, "You're a bloody Pom. I don't have Poms on my squadron – you're posted."

So that was that; within a few hours, my rear gunner Andrew Pike and I were on our way, leaving the rest of my Australian crew behind. We were issued with rail warrants and caught the train to Hull and then changed for the slow connection which would eventually take us to Snaith. The whole journey took about twenty-four hours even though our destination was barely twenty miles away from Breighton. It was very disappointing for our crew to be broken up like that, but such was the authority of a wing commander. I had little time to dwell upon the matter further as Andrew and I reported next day to 150 Squadron at RAF Snaith. However, some time later I was very saddened when I heard that with their new relatively inexperienced Australian pilot, they had gone down over Germany on their third operational trip.

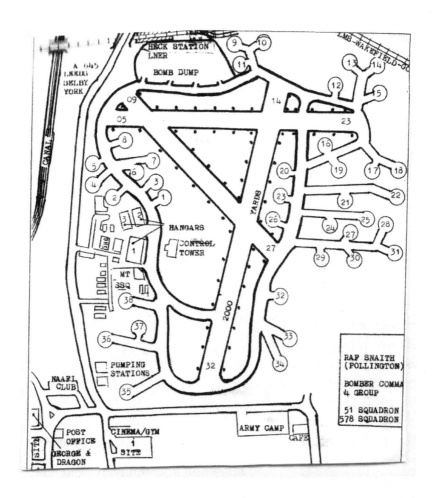

RAF Snaith
[courtesy of Renee Ounsley]

Despite the fact that I had already gained experience in bombing Cologne and Essen as 1st pilot, the CO at Snaith decided I should act as 2nd pilot to other crews to gain more experience. While I was able to do some flying in this role, I was also used as a 'gofer', doing menial tasks such as fetching and carrying coffee and chocolate for other members of the crew, and I felt air sick for the first time in my life. Fortunately, my occupation as a 2nd pilot was very brief.

I now had a new crew, Stan Thomas, Frank Maxfield, Ed Woodruff and Viv Parry. Together we flew a few familiarisation trips round the area, and then began our bombing trips to Germany in earnest. My designated aircraft was a Wellington Mark III with Hercules engines. It turned out to be a very reliable aircraft, and appropriately named 'J for Johnnie'. On the side of the fuselage was painted a picture of 'Jane', the glamorous heroine of a popular comic strip that appeared regularly in the *Daily Mirror*, and whose many adventures inevitably resulted in her parting company with her clothes, much to the approval of the male readership. The aircraft was fitted with Gee radar which enabled the accurate pinpointing of targets as far away as the German Ruhr.

L–R, Self [pilot], P/O Viv Parry [rear gunner], Sgt Frank Maxfield [wireless operator],
Sgt Stan Thomas [navigator] and Sgt Ed Woodruff [bomb aimer/front gunner]
and Jane of course, watching over us!

J for Johnnie in Dispersal. Cpl ■■■■■ in Cockpit.

scan129

J for Johnnie at dispersal

It is important to understand what was involved in every one of the operational trips over Germany. The Squadron would be alerted in the morning that they would be flying on operations that night, whereupon the whole camp would be sealed off: no-one was allowed to enter or leave, no telephone calls could be made, nor was any other form of communication allowed. The only exception was communication between Group Headquarters and the Squadron by means of scrambler telephones. Crews would go out to their aircraft, the pilot would run up the engines, and this would give the navigator the opportunity to test his Gee radar, the wireless operator his radio, the bomb aimer his bomb sight, and the gunners their turrets and guns. After this, the ground crews would fill the aircraft with petrol, bombs and ammunition ready for the trip.

Back at the Mess, after a meal, crews would report to the briefing room. This was a small theatre with a stage and the curtains closed. Crews would assemble, rising when the CO came into the room, after which the curtain was drawn back to reveal a large map of Europe. A ribbon was strung from the airfield to the target for that night, and there were cries of "Cor", "Oh dear" or "Bloody hell" as the target was revealed. The purpose and the importance of the trip were explained. Then came the intelligence information relating to probable opposition from flak and night fighters and details of the target aiming points together with the colours of the Target Indicators that would be dropped in advance by the Pathfinder squadrons. This was followed by meteorological information, technical information and an inspirational talk from the CO. Navigators went away to plot the route in detail, and radio operators received their radio information. Crews then went to the crew-room to pick up their flying helmets, Irvine jackets and trousers, Mae West life jackets, boots, gloves, parachutes, and other paraphernalia. We were then taken by transport out to the various dispersal points around the airfield where the aircraft were parked.

Once ensconced in the aircraft, we waited for the signal to be given, whereupon all the aircraft started up their engines at the same time, the sound of which was thunderous. Aircraft then taxied out onto the perimeter track and lined up one behind the other on the approach to the runway. At the end of the runway stood a 4-wheel caravan with a dome in the top. At a green signal from an Aldis lamp, the first aircraft, which was already positioned at the end of the runway, started to take off. No radio communication was allowed under any circumstances at this point, for fear of attracting the attention of any enemy intruder who might be lurking in the vicinity or of being picked up by long-distance enemy listening stations, so tipping them off that a raid was on its way. As the first aircraft lifted off the ground, its navigation lights were extinguished, and this was the green signal for the next aircraft to start rolling down the runway. In this way, twelve aircraft could be got away rapidly and safely.

All aircraft had a manufacturer's recommended All Up Weight (AUW) for safe flying. This meant that if an engine failed on a twin-engine aircraft, the pilot could still continue to fly safely on the remaining engine. During the war, however, liberties were taken so that from time to time aircraft were loaded above their AUW, and this presented a considerable danger. If an engine were to fail on or immediately after take-off, the aircraft would not be able to maintain height and would be destined to crash immediately – with almost certainly fatal results for the crew.

After a successful take-off, aircraft would climb to around 18,000 feet and head across the North Sea for targets in northern Germany. All down the German, Dutch, Belgian and French coasts was a line of anti-aircraft batteries, which would open fire as our aircraft crossed the coast, sometimes bringing down one or more of our bombers. A further 30 miles inland, a second line of anti-aircraft batteries had to be crossed, after which point we were at the mercy of German night fighters and further flak if we accidentally strayed over a built-up area. It was common to see flak and cannon fire in the night sky and occasionally an aircraft going down in flames – unfortunately usually one of ours.

On arrival at the target, the pilot would open the bomb doors, and the bomb aimer would call directions onto the target – "Steady… steady… left-left… steady… right… steady". If the bomb aimer had set 180 mph and 18,000 feet on his bomb sight it was essential the pilot fly exactly to those figures to ensure the accuracy of the bombing. It took about three minutes to run up to the point of bomb release, plus two minutes for the bomb to fall to the target, and during that time the aircraft was flying straight and level and was exposed to anti-aircraft fire with no defence.

Towards the rear of the aircraft, working under an 8-watt lamp, stood the wireless operator alongside a vertical chute, the bottom of which went through the bottom of the fuselage. When the bomb aimer shouted "Bombs gone!" the wireless operator counted up to three and then pushed a primed 7lb magnesium bomb down the chute. When the main bombs struck the target, the magnesium bomb exploded with a brilliant flash at about 300 feet above the ground, and the shutter of the camera in the aircraft was open, so that a flashlight picture was taken of the bombs striking the target: rather crude, but reasonably effective.

Meanwhile, the Germans on the ground would pinpoint an aircraft with searchlights and fire their 88mm anti-aircraft guns until they shot it down, although latterly they preferred to create an imaginary 'box' over the target area approximately 500 feet deep and a mile square, into which they would continuously fire shells, knowing that all our aircraft must fly through the 'box' to carry out their bombing run. Unfortunately, this method proved much more successful than we would have wished. When the flak was intense and the anti-aircraft shells exploded adjacent to the aircraft, we could hear not only the sharp crack of the explosion but also the shrapnel rattling against the frame of the aircraft as the strong smell of cordite filled the air inside the fuselage. Would the shrapnel hit an engine or damage the control system? Would it set the plane on fire? Worst of all, would it hit the bombs in the bomb bay? That was when our nerves were stretched to the limit.

Over the target, one could see aircraft going down in flames. There were occasional mid-air collisions and cases of aircraft blowing up after being hit by bombs dropped from an aircraft above or having an anti-aircraft shell explode in the bomb bay. This would create a huge fireball which would descend to earth with streamers of fire cascading from it like a giant firework. On moonlit nights the scene became very vivid, and one could see the parachutes descending from stricken aircraft. It was a scene from Hell! It was hoped that the men parachuting down would not be engulfed by the flames below on the ground, although the rising heat coupled with the prevailing wind would probably mean that they would land outside the target area.

All aircrew were known as 'terror fliegers' by the German population, who would think nothing of beating them up, stringing them up on lampposts or even hacking them to death if they caught them. It was rumoured that aircrew caught in the Essen region had been taken to the steel works and thrown bodily into the furnaces alive. The situation was little better if men were picked up by the Geheime Staatspolizei (the Gestapo) or the Schutzstaffel (the SS), by whom they might be tortured or shot. It was hoped they would be picked up by the Wehrmacht (the regular German Army) or local Polizei, in which case they would normally be handed over to the Luftwaffe for civilised interrogation and then sent to a prisoner-of-war camp.

For those still in the air, once out of the target area, aircraft had to deal with German night fighters which would now be circling above waiting for them. And so the homeward-bound journey began, hopefully dodging the night fighters, the anti-aircraft fire and successfully running the gauntlet of the coastal anti-aircraft batteries. Even then, we still had to be careful over the North Sea, because German night fighters would follow as far as they could. Sometimes, pilots had no alternative than to attempt to ditch damaged aircraft in the North Sea. Landing an aircraft on the sea in darkness was extremely difficult and dangerous. If this feat could be accomplished, and if the aircraft did not submerge immediately, it was hoped that the crew would have sufficient time to get out and reach the dinghy that was automatically released on contact with the sea.

In the meantime, hopefully, the wireless operator would have managed to send out a distress signal to be picked up by British radio stations, which could pinpoint their position and send an RAF 'Crash Boat', a high-speed Air–Sea Rescue launch, to pick them up. If aircrew were unable to transmit an emergency signal before ditching then there was little hope for them. If Air–Sea rescue could not get to them first, the next best thing was to be picked up by German naval vessels and taken prisoner because it was not unknown for a dinghy to be found with all the men safely in it but dead from exposure, with their eyes pecked out by seagulls. Air–Sea Rescue did a wonderful job in rescuing crews, sometimes going nearly as far as the enemy coast to pick up survivors.

Back in England, surviving aircraft arrived back at their bases in various forms of disarray, perhaps badly shot-up, whereupon the emergency services would do all they could to help. After landing from every operation, crews always went first for debriefing by the Station Intelligence Officer. Questions were asked about the effectiveness of the bombing, target sighting, enemy activity over the target and en route and return, other aircraft shot down, etc. After discarding flying equipment, it was off to the Mess for their 'flying breakfast' of bacon and eggs. Relieved to be home safely, it was off to bed, sometimes collapsing on the bed through exhaustion.

Aircrew personnel had to make thirty operational trips to complete a tour of duty, but for the young men of RAF Bomber Command, the chances of completing a tour were not good; over 55,000 lost their lives in this long battle in Europe from 1939 to 1945. Bomber Command crews suffered an extremely high casualty rate: 55,573 killed out of a total of 125,000 aircrew (a 44.4% death rate), with a further 8,403 wounded in action and 9,838 more becoming prisoners of war. This covered all Bomber Command operations, including tactical support for ground operations and mining of sea lanes. A Bomber Command crew member had a smaller chance of survival than an infantry officer in the Great War.

As pilot, and therefore captain of the aircraft, there were many times when flying over enemy territory that I felt apprehensive and nervous, bearing in mind the many dangers we faced, but there was no way I could express my feelings in front of my crew; I had to act the fearless leader and provide strength of leadership. Once over enemy territory, it seemed obvious to me that flying straight and level left one open to attack from enemy fighters and anti-aircraft fire. Accordingly, on every trip over enemy-held Europe I developed a weaving motion with my aircraft, consisting of climbing and descending and moving from side to side while maintaining the correct course. Initially, the crew were not very happy with this manoeuvre, which made them feel air sick, but they soon became acclimatised. As a result of adopting this tactic, I only had to resort to an anti-fighter 'corkscrew' manoeuvre twice during the first tour of operations. The instant 'corkscrew' was carried out by the pilot when the rear gunner spotted a German night fighter coming to attack from the rear of the aircraft.

I believe the constant weaving motion denied enemy fighters the chance to 'lock on' to us, and also denied enemy flak batteries the opportunity to gauge our height and direction exactly. However, as I described earlier, when making our final approach and bombing run over the target we were obliged to fly straight and level for a considerable time. At this point, we were very vulnerable, with flak bursting all around us and shrapnel rattling against the aircraft, usually causing some damage. Our nerves were stretched as tight as a bow string, each one of us privately praying that the bomb aimer would quickly release our load of high explosives and incendiaries and let us get out of there as soon as possible. My first three operations with 150 Squadron were to Bremen, which stands on the Weser in northern Germany. This meant flying east from Snaith, out over the North Sea and then crossing the enemy coast at different points on each raid to try to keep the defences guessing which city was the target. It was also important for the bomber stream to stay clear of the string of Frisian Islands where the Germans had flak ships and aircraft based.

As a crew, we made twenty-eight bombing sorties over Germany to cities such as Bremen, Wilhelmshaven, Duisburg, Hamburg, Essen, and Frankfurt and, together with the two 1,000 Bomber raids to Cologne and Essen in May and June which I had done whilst still at OTU, these made up my first tour of thirty ops. Those targets in the heavily defended industrial heartland of the Ruhr, colloquially known to Bomber Command crews as 'Happy Valley', were the worst. There were, though, three exceptions to targets in Germany in my tour: Saint-Nazaire, twice, and Lorient, both on the French Atlantic coast of the Bay of Biscay, where our job was to lay magnetic mines in the harbour entrances leading to the heavily fortified U-boat pens.

These mine-laying operations, known as 'gardening' missions, were far more dangerous than the term suggests. Their object was to lay the mines in the exact positions required to try to prevent the U-boats from entering and leaving the harbours or to restrict enemy shipping movements in certain sea channels, such as the entrance to the Baltic Sea, thus hampering their use of key bases and ports like Kiel. Mine-laying operations took place all the time but particularly during the summer months, in part because of the short nights and the generally better weather conditions. Our first one was to Saint-Nazaire.

As the last rays of daylight slipped away and the darkness closed in on the late evening of 7th July 1942, our small band of

Wellingtons took off from RAF Snaith and headed for Saint-Nazaire. Our course took us south-west to Cornwall and on to the Bay of Biscay so that we would approach the target from the south. Until now, we had been flying at about 10,000 feet, but mine laying was a very low-level operation and I was about to put all those hours of practice to good use. Far out over the waters of Biscay, we began to lose height and the already tense atmosphere in the aircraft palpably increased. We were barely a fortnight past the 21st June, the longest day, and at that time of year, despite the 7/10 cloud cover, it was hardly properly dark. Nevertheless, since our bombing height for laying the mines was to be about 100 feet, even in the dim hue of that shadowy darkness, there was no accurate way of judging the aircraft's position so close above the water; it was pure guess work. What was certain, though, was that it all left precious little room for evasive action if hitting the water was to be avoided, and we knew that the enemy would be waiting for us; they would hear our engines approaching long before we were near the U-boat base.

Then we were skimming across the swelling sea in the approaches to Saint-Nazaire; this was it. My heart was beating faster than I imagined possible. Suddenly, everything around me was bathed in the glorious, deadly white light of the searchlights, followed almost simultaneously by the thumping of the anti-aircraft shells as the defenders sent a curtain of lethal fire horizontally down the beams of light straight at us. The noise was deafening; above the roar of our own engines, I could hear the ack-ack shells exploding above us, beneath us, to the sides, in front and behind us, the red-hot shrapnel rattling against the geodetic frame of the aircraft, ripping holes in the thin canvas sides.

By now, Ed Woodruff had dropped down from the front gun into the bomb aimer's position in the nose of the Wellington, whilst from the rear turret, despite the racket and clamour in the gathering crescendo of explosions and racing engines, I could hear the metallic rattle of our own guns as Viv Parry fired his four Brownings at the lights and the ack-ack batteries beside them that threatened to bring us to destruction.

Searchlights are blinding at such close quarters and to have looked into the beam would have spelled disaster for us as I would have been unable to see anything for many minutes. So, keeping my head down in the cockpit, I concentrated on the instrument panel, trying to maintain height and speed so that Ed could lay the mines in the right position. I was sweating now, sure that at any moment I would feel the Wellington lurch and plunge into the black waves so perilously close beneath me. Then I felt the aircraft lift as Ed's voice in my headset confirmed the release of the mines. Nearly through now; but there was only one way out to safety and we had to keep going through that terrible hail of shells and cannon fire, as we were still too low for me to turn and I dared not climb.

Then, just as suddenly as the cockpit had been filled with light, the darkness folded around us again; this time we were through and the sense of relief was immense. I could scarcely believe that we were still in one piece. I called up each of my crew in turn to check they were all right and to encourage them as we headed back on the long haul home, urging them to keep a sharp lookout for enemy night fighters. At last, and with great relief, we crossed the English coast once more. A little over an hour later, the wheels of the Wellington touched down at RAF Snaith and we were home. Our debrief was followed by the usual operational aircrew breakfast of bacon and eggs and then the blessed relief of bed.

Subsequently the Germans had to send out minesweepers to clear a path through the minefield to let the U-boats in and out of the port. It was a game of cat and mouse which both sides played throughout the war, but it was a game without any fun.

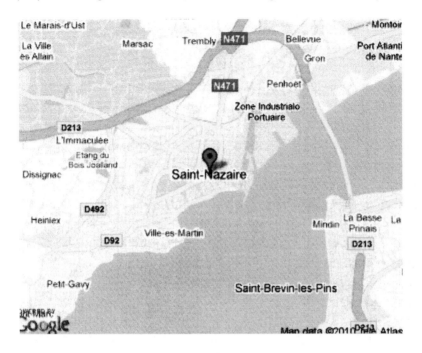

Saint-Nazaire

Before each operational trip I spent two minutes in the cockpit praying for our safe return. This seemed to work. Prayer and the supernatural were part of our family. My maternal grandmother had 'second sight', as it was known in those days, or extrasensory perception (ESP). An example of this occurred one day when she was washing up. She suddenly took off her apron, put on her hat and coat, travelled to the other end of Eastbourne to a house she had never visited before, knocked on the door and told the woman of the house, whom she had never met, that she was to go immediately to Charing Cross Hospital in London, where her husband was critically ill and calling for her. The woman was so persuaded that she caught the next train to London – and arrived in Charing Cross Hospital half an hour before her husband died. My mother had similar powers but to a lesser extent.

I didn't really believe any of this until, while sitting in the Sergeants' Mess on the squadron and watching new replacement crews arriving, I found that I could forecast whether these men would live or die. In time, my predictions would prove to be 100% accurate. It was very disturbing, but I kept these observations, thoughts and conclusions very carefully to myself. But how did this relate to my own circumstances? Every morning as I shaved, I would look in the mirror and contemplate the sobering thought that by the following morning I could be dead, injured or a prisoner of war, yet somehow I felt confident that I would survive. Was it wishful thinking or did I have a guardian angel? I don't know the answer, but I do know that on one occasion, someone or something very definitely helped me to survive.

Duisburg, on the east bank of the Rhine and about ten miles from Krefeld on the west bank, formed one of the gateway entrances to the industrial Ruhr and was heavily bombed during the war, with raids targeting the chemical, iron, steel and logistical centres located there. Like many places in Germany, some of the bombs we dropped on the city had faulty delayed-action fuses, whilst others simply failed to explode as planned and are still being uncovered today, though all now in very fragile condition.

During July 1942 we were listed in the Battle Order for four consecutive raids to Duisburg, the first of which was on the 13th. When we got to the city, there was no more than 5/10 cloud cover and I could see that the defensive flak was frighteningly intense; they seemed to be throwing everything they had up into the sky to prevent us from getting in. The closer to the target area we flew, the more intense the anti-aircraft barrage became; it was the worst I had ever seen and it was immediately ahead of us. Normally, I accepted the danger and flew through it, but at that point, a voice came into my head which said, "If you go into that barrage you won't come out." I heeded the voice and, instead of flying directly through the middle of it as I was supposed to, I flew instead to the outer edge and then released the 4,000lb bomb as I performed a steep turn, leaving centrifugal force to propel it into the target area, whereupon we set off on the homeward-bound leg of our journey and returned safely.

This feeling of a divine guidance never happened at any other time during my operational career. Some may suggest that it was simply a reaction to the intensity of the barrage, but I had flown through intense barrages before and did so again, and the anti-aircraft fire during the mine laying at Saint-Nazaire a few weeks earlier had been immense. Was it a premonition or a supernatural warning? Was it ESP? I will never know, but whatever it was, I have no doubt that I owed my life and the lives of my crew to it. The squadron lost one aircraft that night and I am sure that it would have been two but for my timely warning.

On the afternoon of 6th August, the piece of red tape on the map at the briefing once more led across to Duisburg. It would be Bomber Command's fifth raid to the city in less than three weeks and we had been on them all. As the time for take-off approached, the aerodrome came alive to the sound of engines starting up and aircraft moving out of their dispersal bays. The line of Wellingtons made its way along the perimeter track to the head of the runway and each aircraft was cleared for take-off in fairly quick succession to get the squadron into the air as rapidly as possible so that the runway flare path lights could be turned off in case German intruders were around. The aircraft in front of our own rumbled down the runway, and as soon as it was in the air, we were given the green light from the

Controller's caravan. I released the brakes and J for Johnnie set off between the lights, which flashed past me at increasing speed until finally we too were up and I could no longer see them. I followed the usual procedure and switched off my navigation lights immediately after becoming airborne, but then out of the darkness there came a tremendous explosion and fireball as the aircraft which had taken off a few moments ahead of us hit the ground and blew up.

The flames and debris from the exploding bombs and ammunition were hurled up into the air right in front of us in a massive inferno of burning fuel and lethal shards of fragmented metal. There was nothing I could do but fly straight through it all and pray that no harm would come to our engines. My heart was in my mouth as we plunged into the rising column of fire. The orange and black mass engulfed us, sweeping over our Wellington, which suddenly seemed very flimsy. For those few moments, time stood still. Through the cockpit windows, all I could see was the entrance to the Furnace of Hell. Then the terrible image was gone and J for Johnnie emerged on the other side, seemingly little the worse for wear. I carried out a damage report with the crew and, satisfied that we were still airworthy, we carried on to Duisburg. My prayers had again been answered, but it was an unnerving start to what would be a difficult operation because, unsurprisingly, when we got to the Ruhr, the flak was, as always, very heavy, not just over the target but on the way in and out again.

Five different types of aeroplane made up the 216 on this raid. It was not considered a success, though, as most of the bombs fell in open country to the west of the city. Two Stirlings, two Halifaxes and one Wellington were lost that night; the Wellington was that of our friends who had crashed in front of us on take-off. Subsequently, the cause was found to be the result of the aircraft suffering a catastrophic loss of power in one engine at the critical moment just after take-off and, with a full bomb and fuel load, it had no chance of gaining height on the remaining engine.

On our return from Germany, I called up the control tower at Snaith and asked for permission to land in the normal manner, using my aircraft's call-sign, 'J for Johnnie'. There should have been an instant reply but there was nothing; the airwaves remained open but silent. Then a rather diffident WAAF's voice sounded in my headset and hesitantly asked me to repeat my call-sign; I did and was given a number for landing. I later discovered that, due to the magnitude of the explosion and the intensity of the fire that followed the crash, the people on the ground had been unable to identify which aircraft had come to grief or any of its crew. They had then wrongly concluded that it was J for Johnnie that had blown up because we had been the last aircraft observed to take off immediately prior to the explosion. As a result of this misunderstanding, my crew and I had been written off as killed in action, hence the incredulity upon our safe return; the unfortunate WAAF who received my call-sign thought that she was hearing a voice from beyond the grave. There was much embarrassment all round, particularly as the Adjutant had already ordered ground staff to remove all our personal belongings and clothing from our quarters, which, although the usual procedure for missing and KIA [killed in action] aircrew, was not for aircrew who returned safe and well!

Chapter 9
Tragedy

The pace of raids by the Command did not ease up until mid-August, and on the morning of the 11th we were yet again on the Battle Order. This would be our tenth operation in a little over two weeks; we were getting very tired and feeling the strain; we needed a rest. The target was Mainz in central Germany, the home of the moveable printing press invented by Johannes Gutenberg in 1450.

Over the target, the cloud cover was 5/10 and there was heavy flak. Through the nose of my Wellington, I could see the fires burning brightly in the city streets 15,000 feet below me. We were not troubled by night fighters and returned to Snaith tired, relieved and ready for bacon and eggs, and bed. The squadron lost another aircraft that night and all but one of her crew.

After breakfast next morning, I wandered across to the notice board to look at the Battle Order and, sure enough, there we were: Sgt Trotman and crew. The target turned out to be Mainz again, only this time the weather had begun to deteriorate. Over the target the cloud cover was 8/10 and there was a strong wind blowing. Despite our raid the night before, the flak was still very heavy and I could once more see the fires burning far below me in the industrial areas of the city.

As we started the long flight back to England, I began to grow concerned about our fuel levels. We were never given very much extra fuel in reserve, especially at this stage in the war when the country was desperately short of aviation fuel as the U-boats were taking a daily toll on the supply convoys coming across the Atlantic. I doubted that we had been given short measure back at Snaith; it was more likely that the strong wind had put a strain on the consumption. There was also the possibility that we were losing fuel if a piece of shrapnel had put a hole in a tank. Whatever the reason, as the miles mounted, so did my disquiet. I had not yet told the crew, but I had to do so now. I asked Stan Thomas, my navigator, to give me the shortest course for England and informed everyone about the fuel shortage.

The cloud cover remained stubbornly thick with only occasional breaks, although it did at least help to hide us from fighters. I took the chance and eased back on the engine revs, losing height and using less fuel without the superchargers. It would prolong our time over enemy territory but increase our chances of getting to England and not having to ditch in the Channel. After what seemed an eternity, Stan said that we should be crossing the French coast, and a few moments later, from the front turret, Ed confirmed the coastline slipping beneath us as he glimpsed the breaking waves on the shore through a hole in the clouds. Our fuel levels were now getting to a critical point and I knew that we would not get home to Snaith. The dark waters of the English Channel beckoned beneath us, holding all the perils of a ditching in the dark; something to be avoided at all costs. The minutes ticked by, each one of us praying for the sight of Beachy Head and the safety it would herald if we just had enough fuel to get to an aerodrome with a long enough runway.

I was continuing to lose height but keeping high enough to allow my crew to bail out if they needed to. Then the English coast came up at Beachy Head and, after a quick discussion with Stan, I asked for a QDM [magnetic heading] to RAF Harwell in Oxfordshire; I dared not risk the fuel beyond there. We passed London to our right and began to feel that we would be all right so long as the fuel gauges were accurate. At last, Harwell could be contacted and I asked for permission to come straight in. The wireless operator, Frank Maxfield, fired the Very pistol with the colours of the day and we were given permission to land. It was with immense relief for us all that we felt the wheels touch down on the fairly new concrete runway and J for Johnnie race along between the slowing flare path lights.

We left her on one of the dispersals and reported to the duty officer, who notified Snaith of our safe return. Since this was an operational Bomber Command station, we were easily accommodated with food and a bed. The next morning, with a top-up of fuel, we flew back to Snaith. Once more, the squadron had lost the only Wellington casualty of the night when they had to return to base early but crashed on landing, with the loss of all but one of the crew. We had done well not to have been a second crew lost.

After a short mid-August lull in ops, they had once more become relentless as the nights grew longer. We started September with a raid on the 1st to Saarbrücken, close to the border in south-west Germany. Visibility was very clear and the Pathfinders marked the target well, with the result that it was bombed heavily and accurately. Unfortunately, however, it wasn't Saarbrücken but the small town of Saarlouis, about thirteen miles away, which, from the air at night sitting in an almost identical bend in the river Saar, looked just like the target. Such are the fates of war.

The next night we set out in the same direction, this time going a little further into Germany to Karlsruhe, where we were met by very heavy flak. Our squadron lost one of the four Wellingtons shot down that night. On 4th September, we were again on the Battle Order, the target this time the northern city of Bremen. This would be my twenty-fifth operation. We were getting to the end of our first tour. The bomber stream was routed straight across the North Sea, travelling parallel to the north German coast until it reached a point between Bremen and Hamburg where, to confuse the Germans, we turned inland and then turned again and came up to Bremen from the landward side. The ploy worked, but only for so long. As soon as the enemy realised that Bremen, with its shipyards and Weser aircraft factory, was the real target, the flak batteries opened up with all that they had.

There were 251 aircraft on this raid and in the clear visibility, the target was marked using a new technique for the Pathfinders and one which they would use for the rest of the war. The PFF was split into three groups, the first of which, 'the illuminators', lit the area with white flares. The second group, 'the visual markers', then marked the target with coloured flares once they had identified the aiming point, followed by the third group, who dropped all incendiaries onto the coloured indicators. On our approach to the target, I could see the whole area lit up with many fires already burning fiercely in the city streets below. I began our run-in and opened the bomb doors whilst the familiar sound of Ed's calm voice in the aiming window sounded in my headset as he began to guide me onto the aiming point: "Steady… left-left…right…steady…bombs gone."

The words were barely out of his mouth when there was tremendous double bang under the starboard wing and the aircraft was thrown almost on its back by the force of the explosions. Inside, there was chaos. Ed, hanging on to his bomb sight, was being tossed about in the nose of the aircraft. I hung on tight to the control column, but was fortunately strapped in; Stan was thrown about his little recess, with maps and charts going in all directions; Viv in the rear turret was also fortunately strapped in. However, it was Frank who suffered the most. He was caught in the centre of the aircraft, standing alongside the metal chute ready to count to three and then push the 7lb magnesium bomb for the photograph down the tube. He was thrown off his feet, the primed magnesium bomb flew out of his hand, rolled across the floor and then dropped onto the roof as we almost turned over. At the same time, the lid of the adjacent Elsan toilet flew open and emptied its entire contents all over him.

We were still over the main target area with the rest of the bomber stream around us. I had very little space to work with to avoid a collision and had to use all my skill and experience to bring us safely back onto an even keel. As the aircraft levelled out, Frank scrambled to his feet, slithering and sliding about on the floor in the stinking contents of the Elsan. He picked up the bomb and rammed it back into the chute but his, and our, troubles were far from over. With the seconds ticking away until the magnesium exploded and turned us all into a Roman candle, the bomb stuck in the chute and wouldn't go down; one of its fins had been bent in the mêlée and had caught on the lip of the tube. Frank did what he could to straighten the fin, then hauled himself up by hanging onto the aircraft's internal framework and stamped on the tail of the bomb with his boot, whereupon, much to everyone's relief, it disappeared down the chute and exploded harmlessly outside the aircraft.

After reconnecting himself to the intercom, which had become detached during the fracas, he burst into a tirade of abuse worthy of any navvy, complaining bitterly about being the only one of us to be 'anointed' by the Elsan. I sent the navigator back to see what he could do to help. Frank had been protected to some extent by his helmet, Irvin jacket and boots. The navigator did his best to clean him up, helped him remove his trousers quickly, very quickly, in fact, bearing in mind that the temperature inside the fuselage at that altitude was a cold

-25°C, and wrapped him in blankets taken from the emergency bunk at the rear of the aircraft. Finally, Stan settled him down in the radio recess, where a small heater was able to keep him tolerably warm.

Meanwhile, we had left Bremen behind and were making our way back across the North Sea. I was worried about what damage had been caused to the aircraft and checked the fuel state constantly. It soon became apparent that we were leaking fuel from the starboard tank. These tanks were self-sealing against bullets but not against large pieces of shrapnel. Just as I had done coming from Mainz three weeks earlier, I dropped the aircraft down from 18,000 to 10,000 feet, which enabled me to take out the engine superchargers and so use less fuel. I then put the engines into fast economical cruise to try to ensure that we would get back to England. Every minute seemed like an hour as we droned our way over the North Sea. From the occasional glint of starlight, we could see the black waters far below us, dark, foreboding, treacherous, but they would also lead us to safety. Then, just over halfway home, the starboard engine ran out of fuel; now it really was touch and go whether we would make it back to England at all. I kept the port engine in the cruise mode to conserve fuel but it meant we were gradually losing height, and so, bearing in mind our predicament once more, I told the crew to prepare for the likelihood of a ditching.

The gauge on the port fuel tank was showing that we were almost out of fuel and the sea beneath us seemed very close now. We had practised dinghy drill, but there was no course which allowed us to try out an actual ditching; the first time would be to save our lives. Our height was now just a few hundred feet and slipping away: too low to parachute now. The North Sea was beginning to rush by beneath the aircraft and I knew that we were running out of height quickly. In my mind I went through the drill; thanked God that the sea was calm; imagined the shuddering bang as we hit the water at 90 mph; the spray piling up in front, the aircraft bouncing and then banging down again, hopefully staying level as her last headlong rush was brought to a sudden jarring halt by the wall of water; the sound of the sea rushing into the fuselage as she began to settle. At least the empty bomb bay and fuel tanks would make her more buoyant and give us a few more precious seconds, even minutes, to get out.

Then, in the cold grey light of dawn, the Yorkshire coast appeared out of the murky bulk that was land; we might just make it. We crossed the sparkling line of breakers on the shore with our port fuel tank showing zero and, after flying for about another ten miles, the port engine spluttered, gave a last gasp and stopped; we were gliding from now on. I told the crew to take up their crash positions and looked for somewhere to land. Ahead, I saw a diamond-shaped field which I judged to be big enough for me to get down in.

The controls were getting very heavy now and beginning to shake violently as we rapidly lost height and approached stalling speed. The old Wellington was still just about staying in the air and, with a lot of luck, managed to cross a hedge and belly-land in the field. As she slowed at the other end of the field, the starboard wing-tip clipped a tree, swinging the aircraft round sharply to a 90-degree stop. The three crew who were braced for the crash inside the fuselage quickly vacated the aircraft, but, foolishly, at some time during the flight, I had loosened my harness, and as a result, when the aircraft stopped I was flung forward against the instrument panel, cutting my head in the process. Suffering some concussion and bleeding profusely, rather clumsily I clambered out of the top emergency hatch and joined the other three members of the crew standing on the grass beside our stricken aircraft.

After a minute, I began to recover my senses and asked where Viv Parry was. They led me over to where my rear gunner lay prostrate on the ground. It appeared that when the wing of the aircraft had clipped the tree and spun us round, Viv had been catapulted through the open doors of his rear turret and had broken his neck on the impact when he hit the ground. I stared at him, his face looking placid and peaceful in the death that had come to him so suddenly on English soil when he should have been standing there with us; I burst into tears. What a terrible and tragic thing to happen to one of my crew. I couldn't comprehend it.

I remembered my position as captain of the aircraft and quickly recovered my composure. Although we were all sergeants, I took control and asked Stan to fetch a parachute from the Wellington, open it and cover Viv's body. I then asked Frank, who was still without his trousers, to remain with the aircraft whilst the other three of us set off in different directions to get help. I crossed a fence, then a large field, and came to a canal. The canal was straight, with no bridges in sight, but on the other side of the large field beyond the opposite bank, in the gathering grey light I could see a house. I took off my flying boots and slipped into the cold murky water to wade across the canal, being careful not to be sucked down into the silty bottom. After climbing out on the other side, I put my boots back on and made my way to the house.

I knocked on the door, and after a while, a man appeared in trousers and vest. Still somewhat concussed and slurring my words, I asked him if I could use his telephone. It was still very early in the morning and I had clearly roused the man from his bed, so, given my dishevelled, soaking wet clothes, bleeding head, groggy gait and imprecise speech, it was hardly surprising that he looked at me with a great deal of suspicion, presumably wondering if I might be a German airman rather than the member of His Majesty's Air Force that I claimed to be. I knew that I looked nothing like the commonly portrayed image of a dashing young Royal Air Force flyer returning from operations over Germany, but I finally reassured him that I was indeed with the RAF and on his side. He invited me in, led me to a telephone and then called his wife downstairs. She duly appeared wearing a dressing-gown over her nightie and curlers in her hair, and, being a very practical woman, put the kettle on the stove and gave me a cup of tea laced with whisky. She then filled a bowl with hot water and set about cleaning up my wound, which subsequently required fourteen stitches. During the next few hours, we were all collected from the various houses we had each ended up in, and our aircraft was recovered and taken to a local maintenance depot. After being debriefed about the raid and the circumstances of the forced landing and of how Viv was killed, we were given a week's crash leave.

Squadron Leader Tony Iveson of 617 Squadron once said, "There is nothing more close than a bomber crew. You had to have confidence in each other. Each one had to know his job thoroughly... ...you depended on each other. No matter what difference in rank, as a crew you were a unit and the closer you were the more confidence you had, the better you were." Like many successful crews, we were a very close-knit team and we were deeply saddened by Viv Parry's death, but there was no time or emotional room for mourning; the war carried on as before. On our return from leave, we were allocated a replacement rear gunner and got on with the job. Nevertheless, and no matter how irrational, both at the time and ever since, I have never lost the feeling that I had been responsible for Viv's death. Twenty-seven-year-old Pilot Officer Vivian Weston Parry, DFC, son of John and Eleanor Parry of Comlyn, is buried on the west side of Llanrhwydrys (St Rhwydrys) Church, Anglesey.

Chapter 10
Over halfway

One of the most dangerous activities for the peoples of occupied Europe was to help Allied airmen, soldiers and even sailors to evade capture and escape back to Britain. The civilian men and women who undertook this work were brave beyond measure because the penalty for helping Allied servicemen was ruthless execution by the firing squad, often not only for themselves but for their families as well.

In August 1941, a young Belgian woman turned up at the British Consulate in Bilbao with James Cromar, a British soldier from Aberdeen who had been evading capture since Dunkirk fourteen months earlier. She and Cromar were helped by two Belgian men and had travelled by train from Paris and then on foot over the Pyrenees. It was the start of the Comet Line, perhaps the best-known and certainly one of the most successful escape routes during the war. The young woman and founder of the line was Andrée de Jongh, codenamed Dédée, the 24-year-old daughter of a headmaster in a Brussels school.

After the evacuation of Dunkirk, most evaders were airmen who had been shot down over Europe. The line began in Brussels, where the evaders were fed, clothed and given false identity papers. They were hidden in cellars and attics whilst being passed along a network of trusted people through occupied France into neutral Spain and on to Gibraltar, from where they were flown or shipped back to Britain. After 1942, when southern France was fully occupied under Nazi rule, the work became even more dangerous and many of these courageous people were betrayed, captured, tortured and executed, but the line remained uncompromised. By the end of the war it had saved the lives of over 800 Allied servicemen, 400 of whom de Jongh had personally delivered to safety. With this level of involvement, it was almost inevitable that she would be betrayed, and in January 1943 she was arrested and, over the next few weeks, tortured by the Gestapo. She was sent to the women's concentration camp at Ravensbrück, to the north of Berlin, where some 30,000 women and children were imprisoned. Expected to die or be executed in the camp, Andrée nevertheless survived its horrors and the sadistic officers and guards who brutalised the prisoners. After the war, she returned to Belgium and was awarded the George Medal by the British Government for her immense courage.

One of the pilots on the Squadron with me during my time at Snaith was Sgt Bill Randle. We were both down in the Battle Order for a raid on Essen on the night of 16th/17th September; it would be my second operation after my crash landing, and our replacement rear gunner, Fred Easy, had joined the crew. Bill's Wellington was hit by flak as he crossed the Dutch coast but, despite the damage, he carried on to Essen and bombed the target. However, his Wellington was hit once more, causing the port engine to lose all power. It soon became clear to him that they were not going to get back to England and he ordered his crew to bail out; they were over the Belgian border. Bill landed in a tree, and after extricating himself from its branches and hiding his parachute, he headed for the coast, walking under the cover of darkness. Good luck stayed with him, for he met the right people and was put in touch with what turned out to be the Comet Line. He was interrogated by its members to make sure that he really was who he said he was and then taken, with a new identity, by Andrée de Jongh to Paris, where another young woman took over and led him to the Pyrenees to be met by Florentino, who took him close to the Spanish border. Here, Andrée re-joined the group, led them through the narrow forest paths into Spain and on to Gibraltar.

It took Bill two months to get back to England but his operational days were over. He was awarded the Distinguished Flying Medal, granted a commission, and became an instructor for the rest of the war. The Air Ministry policy was not to allow evaders back onto ops in order to protect those who had helped them escape should they be shot down a second time and captured. Bill owed his freedom, and possibly his life, to the great courage of Andrée de Jongh and her team on the Comet Line. Immediately after the war ended in Europe, he was posted to 692 PFF Squadron, so our paths crossed once again. He subsequently stayed in the RAF, reaching the rank of Group Captain. His extraordinary adventures are recorded in his book *Blue Skies and Dark Nights*.

The same Essen raid which had brought Bill down nearly brought us down too. Crossing the North Sea on our way to Essen that night, we developed an engine fault and I knew that trying to fly on to the target would end in disaster, so, since we were close to Alkmaar airfield not far from Bergen, I decided to bomb that instead. We dropped our load and by catching the German defences completely by surprise, we destroyed a number of aircraft on the ground. We then turned around and flew back to Snaith as fast as I dared with one-and-a-half engines, all the time imagining enraged fighter pilots chasing after us, seeking revenge. Having emptied the bomb bay, the aircraft was much lighter now and that did at least ease the strain on the faulty engine.

Amongst all the death and destruction in the war, there were lighter moments. On the outskirts of the airfield there was a public road on which an elderly wooden bus, well past its prime, ran twice daily. Adjacent to the road was a dispersal point on which an aircraft stood. One day, a new air gunner to the squadron sat testing the function of the gun turret in preparation for operations that night. Without much thought, he loaded ammunition into the breeches of his four Browning machine guns, which were capable of firing 1,000 rounds per minute, lifted off the safety catches and pulled the triggers. Just at that moment, the local bus was passing and, there being no passengers, the conductor was at the front of the bus in conversation with the driver. As the bus passed the stationary aircraft, a stream of bullets entered it just behind the conductor and raked the entire length of the vehicle, reducing it to a splintered wreck. Fortunately, the driver and conductor were unhurt, but, as can be imagined, were more than a little shaken up to have come within a whisker of death and to have had their bus destroyed by the RAF. The crackling sound of gunfire within the aerodrome and the shattering of the bus caused quite a commotion. The air gunner was immediately arrested and never allowed near a gun again, and in due course the company got the Air Ministry to pay for a new bus.

I had taken my £4.19s.6d bicycle with me to Snaith, on which I used to cycle around the camp, until one day, history repeated itself. The front mudguard snagged the front wheel, the bike halted suddenly and I went flying over the handlebars, landed on my head and suffered concussion. I duly reported to the Medical Officer, who decided to keep me in the sick bay overnight. Sometime during the night, I half awoke to find someone feeling my genitals. It was a male orderly. I was not prepared to suffer this indignity, so lashed out with my fist and hit him on the nose, after which I turned over and went back to sleep. Then again, given my confused state of mind at the time, perhaps it was a WAAF orderly? I do hope not! One thing I do know is that my bike was a write-off and I never saw it again, which was probably no bad thing, under the circumstances.

One person who came into the Sergeants' Mess from time to time as a guest was the signalman who worked the signal box at the local railway station. On occasion, a crowd of aircrew going on leave would congregate at the station, whereupon the signalman would set the arm of the semaphore signal at stop and bring the express train running from Edinburgh to Kings Cross, or vice versa, to a screeching, clattering halt at the short platform of this little village station. The aircrew chaps would then scramble aboard and the train would depart, with much muttering and chuttering from the driver and fireman on the footplate, who now had to build up steam and speed once more.

The local village bobby, George, a stout red-faced man, used to ride into the camp every day on his bicycle, visit the guardroom, and call on the Adjutant as the need arose. He would then proceed to the Sergeants' Mess where he would drink his customary free pint of beer. He was an 'honorary member' of the Mess and a frequent visitor. He and his wife also attended Mess parties when WAAF and local girls were invited to drink and dance. As the parties progressed, George could be seen wearing an aircrew blouse, while one member of aircrew would be wearing George's police jacket and another wearing his helmet. At stag parties, everyone would join in drinking beer out of George's helmet, although how it kept its shape nobody knew. At these parties, songs such as 'Salome', 'Roll me over in the clover', 'They say there's a Wimpey just leaving the Ruhr, bound for old Blighty's shore' were sung, with great gusto.

Sometimes when we were stood down from operations, we would go for a night out in Pontefract, Leeds or York. With his frequent visits to the Mess, George was well aware of the heavy losses of young men suffered by the Squadron, seeing familiar faces disappearing and new ones arriving. One evening, there being no operations on that night, four of us decided to go to Betty's Bar in York. One of the chaps had a battered old MG sports car, into which we piled and swept out of the camp gates. Just down the road stood George with his bicycle, and he waved us down.

"Hello, lads, where are thee going then?"

"We're going to Betty's in York, George."

"Aye, I've heard it's reet good. Is yon car taxed?"

"No, George, it isn't."

"Aye, and I don't expect it's insured either?"

"No, you're right."

"And yon exhaust is very noisy and illegal."

"We know, George."

"I bet you've got some funny stuff in yon petrol tank too?"

"You're right again."

Silence. By now we could see our night out coming to nothing. It was clear that George was once again grappling with the moral conflicts of his sworn duty to uphold the law of the land and his loyalty to the boys he loved. Then he took a deep breath and a broad grin spread across his round, ruddy face; he had reconciled his conflict. *"Reet! Bugger off, the lot of you, and 'ave a good time!"*

"Thanks, George – see you back in the Mess later." And off we roared.

Betty's Bar, or 'Betty's Dive', as it was colloquially known, was the downstairs bar of Betty's Tearooms in York, and a great favourite of servicemen and women, particularly the RAF. On one wall, there was a huge mirror on which, during the course of the war, many of these servicemen and women signed their names with the diamond pen provided by the owner, or, alternatively, with some lucky girl's engagement ring. Over the years it grew into quite a collection of names, one or two of which became well known, but all of them brave young men and women. Perhaps the most famous name on the mirror, and certainly one of the most courageous of the war, is that of Norman Jackson, VC, from 106 Squadron. Stationed at Metheringham, just south-east of Lincoln, his aircraft was shot down on 26th April 1944. The mirror is still there today as a tribute to the courage of all these people.

Betty's was founded in 1936 by Frederick Belmont, who, having travelled to America on the maiden voyage of the *Queen Mary* in May that year, was so inspired by the sumptuous art deco surroundings of one of the state rooms that when he returned to York, he engaged the same designers and craftsmen to re-create it in an old warehouse in York and established the legend that was, and remains, Betty's.

A well-known visitor to the bar during my time at Snaith was Jim Harrison, an American from Texas, known, of course, as Tex, who had crossed the border into Canada in order to join the Royal Canadian Air Force (RCAF) as an air gunner and was now stationed at Elvington just outside York. Whenever he came into town, he invariably wore cowboy boots and was forever having difficulties with the RAF Service Police, known throughout the RAF since 1945 as 'Snowdrops' because of their white headgear which was introduced that year, the idea of Group Captain McLaren and Wing Commander Brown.

One night, Tex came into Betty's Dive having had quite a few drinks elsewhere, went to the bar and demanded a whisky. The barman, who knew Tex well, told him that he had had enough to drink, at which Tex became aggressive, pulled out a pearl-handled six-gun from his cowboy boot and pointed it at the barman. He told Tex to put the gun away, but Tex aimed at the back of the bar and promptly shot three bottles of spirits to pieces. At the sound of the shots, the barman ducked down behind the bar, everyone in the room scrambled underneath the tables and two RAF Service Policemen thundered down the stairs to find the cause of the commotion. But when Tex waved his pistol at them, they promptly turned and thundered back up the stairs. Tex then shot another bottle and two lights. Everyone had been counting, and after six shots he was overpowered and the gun taken from him. Thank the Lord that he didn't shoot the famous mirror. The Service Police then thundered back down the stairs once more, arrested him and took him back to his camp.

His Commanding Officer reprimanded him and confined him to camp. Tex was in a unique position. He was still an American citizen and could quit the RCAF at any time. He was also a very good air gunner, and his squadron were loath to lose him. As it was, he completed a tour of thirty operations with his squadron, and then re-mustered to the United States Army Air Force, where he was immediately promoted to the rank of captain and sent back to America to run gunnery training courses.

There were three identifiable periods in a crew's tour when they were even more likely to fail to return [FTR] than normal; the first four or five trips as they began to gain experience, the middle point when complacency had to be avoided, and the last few, when the looming prospect of survival made crews nervous and jittery. We were no different: the second half of September brought our last three ops. Maintaining the discipline that had served us so well, praying to God and hoping for our good luck to continue were all we could do. Above all else, though, it was good luck that brought crews through; without it, a crew was doomed.

On 18th September, two nights after the Essen mission when we had bombed Alkmaar airfield, we were part of a force of 115 Lancasters, Stirlings and Wellingtons tasked to lay mines over a vast area at opposite ends of Europe, from Lorient at the northern end of the Bay of Biscay to Danzig on the Baltic coast. For 150 Squadron, the target was Lorient, one of the main U-boat bases from where they were putting to sea and ravaging the ships and men of the Merchant Navy, who were giving their all to bring the desperately needed supplies across the Atlantic from America and Canada.

The cloud cover was 5/10 over Biscay, which helped us somewhat, but all too soon, the searchlight and flak batteries opened up. They had no trouble picking us out at 100 feet above the water and the horizontal fire was even heavier than it had been at Saint-Nazaire back in July. Our aircraft was hit, although fortunately not in any vital part, and the crew were uninjured. Once Ed Woodruff had told me that the mines were laid, I increased the power on the Wellington's engines and got us out of there as quickly as possible. It had been an even closer call than at Saint-Nazaire and I had the feeling that we were pushing our luck.

We were down for ops again the next night; it was Saarbrücken once more, this time above 10/10 cloud and we bombed by dead reckoning through it. It was my twenty-ninth mission; just one more to go. We were all getting jittery; when would the last one be and where?

We didn't have long to wait; our thirtieth and final operation came on 23rd September and was a second trip to Saint-Nazaire to drop magnetic mines in the U-boat channels. The weather had taken a definite turn for the worse around the autumn equinox and large raids were not undertaken. Instead, Bomber Command sent out small groups of aircraft to a variety of targets.

The light had faded early, and in the steady drizzle that swept across the aerodrome of RAF Snaith and soaked everything it touched that early autumn evening, the handful of crews from 150 Squadron chosen for this mission were each gathered around their aircraft; final checks, a few words of assurance from the ground crew, sign for the aeroplane, scramble aboard out of the wet and then it was time to go. Too many crews came to grief on their last op; we prayed we wouldn't be another one.

Line astern, the aircraft moved around the perimeter track to the runway. We were part of a very small force of twenty-five Wellingtons and eight Stirlings without Pathfinders on gardening ops that night. Presently, I got the green light from the Controller and released the brakes; we began to roll down the concrete for our last op. Dear God, bring us back safely. Our route took us south-west over the Peak District, on down to Bristol, across Devon and into the Western Approaches. Here we swung further west before turning south, then east then north-east to come in to Saint-Nazaire from the south-west. It was the same course that we had taken ten weeks earlier on 7th July, but that seemed a lifetime away now.

Saint-Nazaire had become very heavily defended since the audacious raid, codenamed *Operation Chariot*, on 28th March 1942 by the Royal Navy and Royal Marine Commandos when HMS *Campbeltown*, crammed full of delayed-action high explosives, was rammed into the gates of the *Normandie* dry dock, where it exploded later that day, putting the dock out of action until well after the war and thus denying Atlantic dry dock facilities to the German battleship *Tirpitz*, sister of the destroyed *Bismarck*. It was a raid in which Wellingtons of 150 Squadron had also taken part.

For now, the cloud and drizzle that had cloaked Yorkshire had been left behind and we had flown into clearer skies, although the sea beneath us was still rough. The night was early in the September moon period and the clear visibility helped me to judge how close to the sea we were flying on our run-in, but it also showed us up to the defenders, who picked out our approach against the lighter sky.

This was our third mission against the U-boat bases and we knew exactly what was waiting for us down there. Lower and lower I brought the Wellington, down to 100 feet. We flashed over the troubled waters of Biscay, dark and threatening, the white horses gleaming in the pale moonlight, siren salutations enticing us to join them in eternity.

On we flew, closer to our target area to lay the mines. I could feel my heart rate increasing, waiting for the inevitable as we closed the enemy. Then, as if a switch had been flicked on, the sky around me erupted into a cauldron of fire and light, of cordite and orange shell bursts. The searchlights caught us almost immediately and the flak batteries pumped death and destruction at us. At a hundred feet above the sea, the cockpit was washed in a brilliant white light but even in the dazzling glare of the searchlight beams I could see the glowing balls of flak streaking towards us and zipping past, rocking the Wellington, spraying it with shrapnel and tearing gaping holes in the fabric.

The defenders were trying their best to blast us out of the sky with a lethal hail of light flak sent horizontally down the searchlight beams. So close to the sea and to the guns, the noise inside the aircraft was deafening. Concentrating on the instruments before me, I struggled with all my strength against the terrible buffeting we were getting to keep the aircraft straight and level for Ed. The mines were going in; we were almost done. And then, just as the last one slipped out of the bomb bay, there was a great crash behind me and a blast of cold air. A hole had been blown in the side of the aircraft, but, fortunately, there was no fire and no injuries; incredibly, our luck still held.

Then we were through, into darkness and on the way home. Again we swung out towards the Atlantic and up into the Western Approaches before retracing our route home. As I lowered the undercarriage that morning I was very conscious that we might have had a tyre burst in all the flak that we had taken. I warned the crew to be prepared for a rough landing and brought the Wellington in for the last time. Slowly, she sank towards the earth, hesitated, then touched the concrete; I held my breath. We were down and racing along the flare path, each light passing more slowly than the last; it was over, our luck had indeed held, for the tyres were fine. On our safe return from this sortie, the sense of relief and easing of pressure we all experienced was immense. At that time, fewer than 25% of aircrews completed a full tour of thirty operational trips; the survival rate was appallingly low. We held a celebratory party and were subsequently dispersed to various stations round the country to take up posts as instructors. It was in that capacity that I was posted to No.81 Operational Training Unit (OTU) Tilstock. It was the end of September 1942.

In the world at large, 1942 had been a traumatic year, starting with the fall of Singapore to the Japanese. Closer to home, the U-boat menace was having its effect, with over three million tons of shipping being sunk between January and July. There was some good news from the Pacific, however, with the American naval victory at the Battle of the Coral Sea, which decimated part of the Japanese fleet. There were also tentative signs of the war turning in our favour following the news of the 8th Army's success at El Alamein.

It was during 1942 that Air Chief Marshal Arthur Harris had assumed control of Bomber Command, which had a total strength of around 500 bombers at that time. The old Whitley, Blenheim, Hampdens and other obsolete bombers were being replaced with Halifax and Lancaster aircraft and the new de Havilland Mosquito was now being sent to squadrons. Additionally, the Pathfinder Bomber Force was set up under the control of Air Vice-Marshal Bennett, who had early in the war been shot down over Europe and managed to evade capture.

Plaque at Snaith Memorial

Snaith Memorial

Squadron and Log Book Entries for my first tour of Operations

23 OTU Pershore, Worcestershire

Date	Aircraft	Target	Remarks
30.05.42	Wellington Ic	Cologne	1st 1,000 bomber raid. Vis clear, flak overwhelmed
01.06.42	Wellington Ic	Essen	2nd 1,000 bomber raid. Cloud 8/10. Krupp's factory hit. Me110 claimed shot down. Heavy flak.

No.150 Squadron, Snaith

Date	Aircraft	Target	Remarks
24.06.42	Wellington 3	Bremen	Vis clear. Docks bombed. Heavy flak, a/c holed
29.06.42	Wellington 3	Bremen	Cloud 10/10. Bombed on dead reckoning & Gee radar. Heavy flak. [3 a/c lost from Sqn]
02.07.42	Wellington 3	Bremen	Vis clear. Haze over target. Bombed on dead reckoning &

			Gee radar. Heavy flak.
07.07.42	Wellington 3	St Nazaire	Cloud 7/10. Laid magnetic mines into river estuary from 100 feet to deter U-boats entering & leaving port. Intense flak fired horizontally with aid of searchlights.
08.07.42	Wellington 3	Wilhelmshaven	Vis clear. Bombed port. Heavy flak.
13.07.42	Wellington 3	Duisburg	Cloud 5/10. Bombed target. Intense flak. [1 a/c lost]
21.07.42	Wellington 3	Duisburg	Cloud 7/10. Bombed with incendiaries. Many fires. Intense flak.
23.07.42	Wellington 3	Duisburg	Cloud 6/10. Bombed target. Heavy flak.
25.07.42	Wellington 3	Duisburg	Cloud 7/10. Bombed with incendiaries. Many fires seen. 1

			a/c abandoned trip > heavy icing. 1 a/c abandoned trip > turret fault. [1 a/c lost]
26.07.42	Wellington 3	Hamburg	Vis clear. Bombed target in docks. Very heavy flak. a/c holed. [1 a/c lost]
29.07.42	Wellington 3	Saarbrücken	Cloud 7/10. Bombed with incendiaries. Many fires. Heavy flak.
01.08.42	Wellington 3	Düsseldorf	Cloud 5/10. Bombed target. Intense flak.
04.08.42	Wellington 3	Essen	Cloud 10/10. Bombed on dead reckoning & Gee radar. Heavy flak. Heavy icing in cloud. 6 a/c abandoned trip > heavy icing.
06.08.42	Wellington 3	Duisburg	Cloud 10/10. Bombed on dead reckoning & Gee radar. Heavy flak. 1 a/c crashed on

			take-off [4 dead]; 1 a/c abandoned trip > technical fault.
09.08.42	Wellington 3	Osnabrück	Cloud 7/10. Bombed target. Moderate flak.
11.08.42	Wellington 3	Mainz	Cloud 5/10. Target clear on river. Many fires. Heavy flak. 1 a/c returned to Coltishall & crashed [4 dead]; 1 a/c abandoned trip > engine fault.
12.08.42	Wellington 3	Mainz	Cloud 8/10. Bombed with incendiaries. Many fires. Heavy flak. 1 a/c abandoned trip > engine fault. 1 a/c returned to base & crashed [4 dead]; own a/c returned to Harwell after trip > fuel shortage.
24.08.42	Wellington 3	Frankfurt	Cloud 4/10. Bombed with incendiaries. Many fires. Heavy flak. 2 a/c returned

			after trip to other airfields > fuel shortage. [3 a/c lost].
27.08.42	Wellington 3	Kassel	Vis clear. Thick ground haze. Many fires. Heavy flak. [1 a/c lost]
28.08.42	Wellington 3	Saarbrücken	Cloud 7/10. Target hit. Heavy flak. Numerous German fighter attacks. 2 a/c returned after trip to other airfields > fuel shortage.
01.09.42	Wellington 3	Saarbrücken	Vis clear. Target hit. Many fires. Moderate flak.
02.09.42	Wellington 3	Karlsruhe	Cloud 6/10. Target hit. Very heavy flak. [1 a/c lost]

04.09.42	Wellington 3	Bremen	Vis clear. Target hit. Many fires. Very heavy flak. 1 a/c returned after trip & crashed [1 injured]. Own a/c hit over target. Returned on 1 engine & crashed in Yorkshire field [1 dead] [2 a/c lost]
14.09.42	Wellington 3	Wilhelmshaven	Vis clear. Ground haze. Bombed with incendiaries. Many fires. Heavy flak.
16.09.42	Wellington 3	Essen	Cloud 2/10. Ground haze. A/c had engine fault. Bombed Alkmaar airfield. Several a/c destroyed. 3 a/c abandoned trip > engine faults [1 a/c lost]
18.09.42	Wellington 3	Lorient	Cloud 5/10. Laid magnetic mines into river estuary from 100 feet to deter U-boats entering & leaving port. Intense

			flak fired horizontally with aid of searchlights. Own a/c hit.
19.09.42	Wellington 3	Saarbrücken	Cloud 10/10. Bombed on dead reckoning & Gee radar. Heavy flak. 1 a/c abandoned > engine failure. 2 a/c returned after trip to other airfields > fuel shortage.
23.09.42	Wellington 3	St Nazaire	Vis clear. Laid magnetic mines into river estuary from 100 feet to deter U-boats entering & leaving port. Intense flak fired horizontally with aid of searchlights. A/c holed.

Armstrong Whitworth Whitley
[courtesy of Wikipedia]

CHAPTER 11
No.81 Operational Training Unit, Tilstock, Shropshire

No.81 OTU was a new airfield located near Whitchurch in Shropshire. The airfield had originally been called RAF Whitchurch Heath but since there are at least seven towns named Whitchurch in Britain, and in order to avoid confusion, it was decided to rename it after a local village, Tilstock. The airfield was actually located on Prees Heath, which during the First World War had been a large army camp, complete with hospital and cinema. It subsequently reverted to agricultural and common land before being taken over by the RAF. The airfield was built by McAlpine and covered the main A41 road. A new A41 diversion road therefore had to be built to the south of the airfield to link up with the A49.

A few miles down the road, another new airfield was built at Sleap near Wem, and this acted as a satellite airfield for Tilstock to enable the high volume of flying training to be handled. The aircraft in use were Armstrong Whitworth Whitley Vs, retired from active bombing service. They had Rolls Royce Merlin engines, were relatively slow and cumbersome, needed strength to handle the controls but were docile and reliable in performance.

Audrey and Sonia now re-joined me and we lived out in digs in Whitchurch, with me commuting into the camp daily. At this OTU we assembled crews consisting of pilots, navigators, wireless operators, bomb aimers/front gunners and rear gunners, drawn from their various training courses. Initially, pilots were trained to be competent to fly the aircraft, and then the crews joined in so that cross-country and bombing practices, both day and night, could be carried out as a team, at first under supervision and then on their own.

At this time, I was sent for an interview with a Commission Board with a view to being promoted to officer rank. The interview went satisfactorily, but I had a problem with the medical examination. It was established that I suffered from some colour-blindness, and I was told I could no longer fly. I appealed against this, on the basis that I could distinguish the colours red, green, white and amber; I also pointed out that I had just completed a full tour of operations without having confused any colours of the day or TIs. It was finally decided that, whilst I confused some greens with blues, I was safe and could therefore continue flying. Colour recognition was a very important attribute for wartime pilots because it enabled them to recognise such items as navigation lights, marker flares, and the signal lights located at the beginning of the runway. These signal lights were arranged to show an aircraft red if his approach was too low, green if he was on the correct flight path, and amber if he was too high.

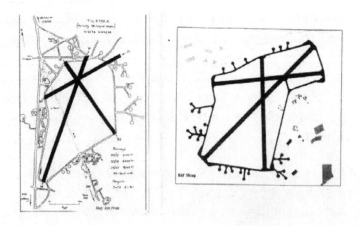

RAF Tilstock [left] & RAF Sleap
Reproduced courtesy of Langrist Caiger Publishers

My conversion to Whitleys lasted two hours, after which it was decided I could instruct. The airfield at Tilstock had three runways, one long and the other two relatively short. The short south-west/north-east runway was intersected by the perimeter track: in other words, the runway extended beyond the perimeter track. This meant that cyclists, vehicles and aircraft travelling around the perimeter track would need to cross the runway at this point. To avoid accidents they were required by standing orders to halt at a painted line some 50 feet short of the runway and look carefully both ways to ensure that no aircraft were using the runway to take off or land before attempting to cross.

One day, I was teaching a pilot to land and he was making a satisfactory approach to the short south-west runway. I had noticed a four-ton lorry approaching the runway on the perimeter track on my side of the aircraft and naturally assumed it would halt as required at the painted line until it was safe to cross. To my horror, just as we were touching down, I saw the lorry continue onto the runway; we were going to crash! In that moment, I wrenched the controls off the trainee pilot, opened the throttles wide, bounced the aircraft on its large balloon tyres, hauled back on the control column and, with the aircraft staggering into the air, cleared the lorry by about two feet. I then throttled back and landed the aircraft. My heart was pounding; it had been a close shave! Looking back, I could see that the truck was unharmed and had stopped just off the runway. My pupil was as white as a sheet with the shock that certain death had stared us in the face. He calmed down and we carried on the landing practice session, at the end of which I sent him off to fly solo to give him confidence and take his mind off our near disaster. On return to the flight office, I rang the transport section to find out who had been driving the lorry.

Shortly afterwards, a WAAF reported to me and said she was the driver of the lorry and was sorry for what had happened. It appeared the other WAAF in the truck with her was in tears due to trouble with her current boyfriend and the driver was trying to placate her. Her manner was casual, and this annoyed me. I shouted at her to stand to attention and then berated her in no uncertain terms. I described in detail what would have happened if the aircraft and the truck had collided. With the aircraft travelling at 70 mph, she and her companion could have been killed in one of three different ways: the steel propeller blades would have chopped them up along with the lorry cab; the lorry cab would have been crushed by the force and weight of the aircraft; or thirdly, the lorry would have been forced sideways along the runway, the tyres ripped off and the steel wheel rims showering sparks off the concrete, petrol from the split petrol tank of the lorry would have ignited and the lorry and aircraft engulfed in a fireball, resulting in the death of the two WAAFs and the two pilots. I then told her in detail what burnt, blackened and charred bodies looked like.

I admit I gave the girl a hard time, but she still didn't seem to understand the gravity of what she had done. I then said I would not have her driving a lorry again, and finally the result of her misdeed registered and she burst into tears. She went away looking green and tearful. I subsequently received a telephone call from the Transport Officer about the way I had treated his staff, but I was in no mood to give way even though he outranked me.

This incident reawakened memories of my first tour on an operational squadron. Since coming off operations, I had suffered nights when I would suddenly shoot up in bed shouting and perspiring, though thankfully this gradually wore off. This was caused by a combination of mental pressure, plus visions of seeing comrades killed in exploding aircraft in the air or seeing the results of air crashes by burning or exploding aircraft on the ground. Not all the fatalities occurred over Germany.

After basic training, we flew with complete crews on bombing range exercises and cross-country exercises. One of the routes for cross-countries was Whitchurch – Prestatyn – Mull of Galloway – Isle of Man – Anglesey – Whitchurch. On one occasion, a layer of cloud covered most of the route, so navigation had to be done with radio fixes, compass and watch, known as dead reckoning. On nearing base, the navigator instructed the pilot to lose height, and at this, the trainee pilot prepared to dive down through the cloud without a thought. Naturally, I stopped him from carrying out such a foolish manoeuvre without knowing exactly where he was. There were hills to the west and south of Whitchurch, and it would have been easy to crash into them if the base of the cloud was low. So I taught him how to locate the airfield and land safely using the 'blind flying beam system'.

The Beam Approach System comprised a transmitter mast located at the windward end of the main runway which emitted a narrow but widening radio beam of a constant hum along the length of the runway and beyond for about six miles. It also emitted a similar hum 180 degrees in the opposite direction, but weaker and not so far. On one side of the beam a series of dots was transmitted, and on the other side dashes were transmitted. This meant that knowing the direction of the runway and therefore the beam, it was possible to know your position relative to the beam. Additionally, directly over the transmitter was a 'cone of silence', which indicated you were exactly over the end of the runway.

If, flying above the airfield in cloud, for example at 1,000 feet, a pilot intercepted the beam, he could fly down it until he reached the 'cone of silence', then turn 90 degrees left and fly for one minute (at 120 mph that would be two miles), turn left 90 degrees and fly for two minutes (four miles) then, lower his undercarriage, turn left 90 degrees, lower the flaps, and at just over one minute turn left 90 degrees onto the beam, with the runway one mile long, the pilot would know he had three miles to go to the beginning of the runway, so that at 90 mph (one-and-a-half miles per minute) he had two minutes to descend 1,000 feet, or 500 feet per minute, to arrive safely at the beginning of the runway.

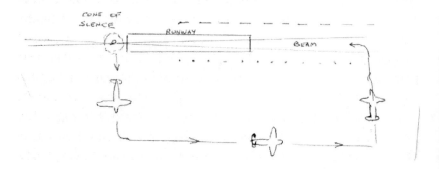

Beam approach

The above example indicates the need for fast mental arithmetic whilst flying an aircraft on instruments in cloud. Today, of course, pilots have computers and the Instrument Landing System (ILS).

A similar incident occurred to me on a night cross-country exercise with cloud covering the whole of the north-west and Irish Sea, when a trainee navigator advised the trainee pilot to lose height immediately after leaving Anglesey for Whitchurch. In this case, I stopped the pilot losing height and made the navigator review his chart workings. The navigator still thought he was right, until I managed to convince him that if we had followed his instructions we would all have been dead, having flown into the mountains of Snowdonia. I had to have hard words with him for poor navigation, and with the pilot for obeying the navigator's instructions without questioning them. Rigorous training was necessary to avoid accidents.

Another night, I took up a pilot and his crew to practise night landings. We commenced flying about midnight and the pupil pilot was doing quite well. In the Whitley the undercarriage was retracted by pulling backward on a floor-mounted lever which returned to the vertical position when the undercarriage was locked up. On the downwind leg in this case, the pilot attempted to push the lever forward to lower the undercarriage but found that the lever was still locked in the rear 'up' position. No matter what we tried, the lever would not move. I got on the radio, and the Engineering Officer was fetched out of his bed. At his suggestion, we tried various techniques, most of which we had already tried, but to no avail. We then reverted to the emergency system whereby the undercarriage could be lowered by hand. A cranked handle was inserted onto a shaft located on the inside of the fuselage, one on each side of the aircraft for each of the main wheels, and in this way the port wheel was successfully lowered and locked. The starboard wheel, however, would not budge. So now we were stuck, with one main wheel up and one main wheel down.

After checking our fuel situation, I decided we would remain airborne carrying out navigation exercises until dawn, and only when daylight came would I attempt to make a landing. I had decided to land on the grass alongside the right of the main runway; so at first light I informed ground control what I proposed to do.

I ordered the crew to their crash positions and brought the aircraft in to land, touching down on the port-side main wheel, holding up the starboard wing as long as possible before it dropped to the ground, whereupon the aircraft swung 90 degrees to the right and stopped. After coming to a halt, we vacated the aircraft promptly, thankful to still be in one piece.

We had been followed by the fire engine and the ambulance of the crash crew, but happily they were not necessary. The aircraft was subsequently jacked up, the faulty undercarriage wheel was lowered, and it was towed away. After the ground crew had replaced the propeller and repaired the hydraulics, the aircraft was flying again after two days.

In the immediate area of Whitchurch it was estimated that there were over thirty pubs and, bearing in mind the town had a population of only 7,000 people, this represented plenty of choice. The Raven on Prees Heath was popular and many RAF people met there to drink. A lesser known pub out on the Wem road was the Harp. This was frequented by American soldiers stationed at Wem and the proprietor was well known. At closing time he closed the front bar in the pub, but if you went to the back you could still gain entrance. It was to this pub that my ex-wireless operator Frank Maxfield and I took a young pilot officer to celebrate his 21st birthday. His parents had been killed in an air raid, and his only brother had been killed at sea, so he was orphaned with no close family. With the help of the publican at the Harp, we gave him an evening that he remembered for the rest of his tragically short life. He later returned to operations and was killed when his aircraft crashed, still only twenty-one.

Another pub in the area was called the Bull and Dog. It had a small bar and a snug with high wooden benches surrounding an open fire. The rest of the building was a barn which contained hay. The bar had a zinc top and when you asked for a beer, Gerald Lyman, the proprietor, would go down into the cellar, draw beer from a barrel and bring it back up to the bar in an enamel jug from which he would pour it into a glass. It was excellent beer.

During my stay at Tilstock I decided I needed my own transport. One night when visiting a pub in Greenend in Whitchurch, I happened to notice in a stack yard adjacent to the pub a little pre-war Ford 8 half-buried under straw, with hens pecking around it. I negotiated with the landlord and bought the car for the princely sum of £5. I went back later, took out the plugs, injected penetrating oil, made sure the engine would turn over, checked the oil, cleaned the plugs, put petrol in the carburettor, connected a torch battery to the coil and the engine started up. I drove that car for many miles, its only drawback being that when the car reached 35 mph the passenger door had a tendency to fly open, much to the dismay of any front-seat passenger. The front doors on this model were hinged at the rear!

A well-known character at Tilstock was Sinbad, a white, battle-scarred bull terrier. He had once belonged to a squadron leader on the camp and was now resident, doing the rounds of the various messes to get his meals. Most evenings he would catch the early local bus into Whitchurch, occupying a seat from which he refused to be ejected, to visit his girlfriends, and he would always manage to catch the last bus back into camp. He was reported having been seen as far away as Crewe, Liverpool and Manchester, though whether this was really true, it was difficult to say. He enjoyed the company of men in blue but hated men in khaki.

The Station Warrant Officer [SWO], a long-serving airman whose career had begun 'before Pontius was a pilot', was responsible to the Station Commander for the discipline and welfare of all non-commissioned ranks. This man was large and rotund, with a substantial beer belly and a loud voice that could be heard at some distance. He had a nasty temper, and took every opportunity to publicly demean men of whatever rank and in a loud voice. He was feared and hated by all non-commissioned ranks and he was particularly disliked by NCO aircrew, all of whom he regarded as upstarts.

Wartime aircrew, because of the nature of their job and their limited life expectancy, were given accelerated promotion. After six months, an aircrew sergeant would be promoted to flight sergeant, and after a further year, he would be given the rank of warrant officer, though aircrew warrant officers were as rare as hens' teeth. Officers were initially appointed as pilot officers, then after six months were promoted to flying officer and, after a further year, were made up to flight lieutenant. Thereafter, promotion through the officer ranks came by filling 'dead men's shoes'.

One day, when walking through the camp, I was wearing my forage cap in my shoulder epaulette instead of on my head. This resulted in a shouted public reprimand from the SWO in front of other ranks, much to my annoyance and embarrassment. I realised I had disobeyed the rules by not wearing the cap, but the reprimand could have been made with a quiet word.

At about this time, I had become concerned that, after more than two years, I was still a sergeant and that I had heard nothing following my interview for a commission. Accordingly, I went to the Adjutant, who promised to investigate the situation. A few days later, he called me into his office and informed me that the reason for my non-promotion was because I was dead! Apparently, another airman who was my namesake had been killed earlier in the war but RAF Records at Uxbridge had 'pulled' my records instead of his. It seemed that Records had been busily promoting the dead man instead of me. Thereafter things moved rapidly as my records caught up. Two days later, I was confirmed as a flight sergeant, backdated, and this was quickly followed by my becoming a warrant officer. Then my commission was confirmed, and because that was backdated, I missed being a pilot officer and automatically became a flying officer. I suspect that was the fastest promotion through the ranks in the history of the RAF; all in one week!

Shortly afterwards, I was walking through the camp when the SWO passed me without a glance. I could not resist the temptation. I shouted after him, beckoned him to me and demanded to know why he had not saluted an officer. SWOs did not normally salute junior officers, only when on formal parades, but RAF regulations stated that all NCOs should salute officers, and I decided this should apply. His face went beetroot red and he gave me a barrack square salute. I thanked him, returned the salute and dismissed him. I had not realised that this event had been witnessed, and word soon spread throughout the camp, much to everyone's amusement, with the result that the SWO, now feeling his position in the camp was untenable, asked for a transfer. He was replaced by another SWO who, while a disciplinarian, was both firm and fair.

As an officer, one had from time to time to be the Duty Officer of the Day. On one occasion, all the sergeant pupils were drawn up on parade, and while walking along the front row carrying out my inspection, I was astonished to see two of my old school pals, Johnnie Rolland and Ken Holman. After the parade was dismissed, we met and talked. They told me they had originally joined the Army, but had re-mustered into the RAF as aircrew when the opportunity arose and were now on their way through the training programme. I was very pleased to see them; we had all come a long way from Aldershot County High School. Happily, they both survived the war too.

Whilst in Whitchurch, I was visited by my sister Marjory and her RAF husband, whom she had married while in India. They had only recently returned to England, and I had not seen her since she had left for India many years before. I was very glad to see her after such a long time, but we were destined never to meet again. Marjory was about seven months' pregnant with her first child at the time of her visit and later went into hospital in Aldershot, where sadly she died of septicaemia. The baby, David, survived and was raised by my sister's brother-in-law and his wife.

Marjory

It was whilst Audrey and I were living in Whitchurch that our marriage broke down. We had married very young, and over the three years since, many things had changed. I was no longer a young naïve lad of 19; I had been hardened by my experiences of life and death, and had gained maturity by being put in charge of other men. In addition, the tension and pressure of my squadron duties had made me restless and unable to settle down to routine domesticity. We separated, and Audrey returned to Farnham to live with her parents. It was a sad time and I felt terribly guilty about deserting my daughter Sonia.

Training continued intensively, but there were many casualties. During my time at Tilstock, there were numerous accidents, as the following list confirms:

Date	Aircraft	Accident	Casualties	
			Killed	Injured
30/11/42	Whitley	Crashed	2	1
11/1/43	Whitley	Crashed	8	
-/-/43	Whitley	Engine failure	1	
10/4/43	Whitley	Crashed	1	3
11/4/43	Whitley	Crashed	1	
13/4/43	Whitley	Engine failure	7	
17/4/43	Whitley	Crashed	2	2
28/4/43	Whitley	Engine failure		2
-/5/43	Whitley	Crashed	5	
13/5/43	Whitley	Crashed	1	4
21/6/43	Whitley	Crashed	1	4
2/7/43	Whitley	Engine failure		
13/7/43	Whitley	Crashed	6	
Total:			35	16

In addition, during this period, there were accidents at Sleap, our satellite airfield, as follows:

Date	Aircraft	Accident	Casualties	
			Killed	Injured
2/5/43	Whitley	Crashed	5	
26/8/43	Whitley	Crashed into control tower	2	12
2/9/43	Whitley	Crashed	5	
7/9/43	Whitley	Crashed into control tower	6	4
6/11/43	Whitley	Crashed		
9/11/43	Whitley	Crashed		
Total:			18	16

Building upon the success of El Alamein, events had moved fast in 1943 and the tide of war began to turn against the Nazis. Guy Gibson and the Dambusters of 617 Squadron had breached the Möhne and Eder Dams in May, Sicily had been invaded, followed by Italy in September. By the end of the year, Italy had surrendered to the Allies, although the Germans moved in to replace them, providing strong resistance to the Allied advance. To further improve the accuracy of RAF bombing, a radar system called *Oboe* had been introduced, which helped to pinpoint targets more accurately. Hamburg was severely damaged, and Berlin now became a regular target.

It was at this time that changes were to be made at RAF Tilstock. Glider-towing was introduced, initially using Whitleys as tugs, and then with the larger redundant four-engine

Stirlings. I was posted to RAF Peplow, another relatively new airfield not many miles away. It was January 1944.

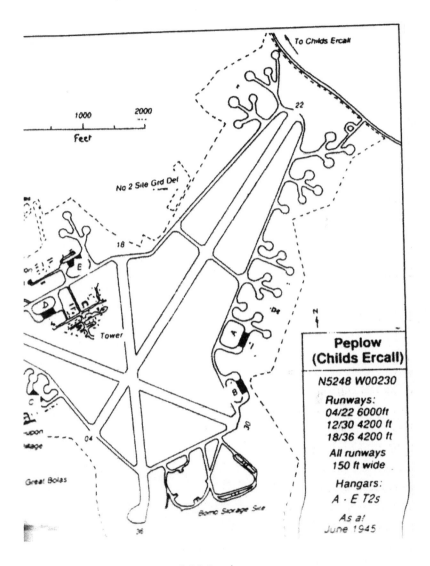

RAF Peplow
[courtesy of Langrist Caiger Publishers]

CHAPTER 12
No.83 Operational Training Unit, Peplow, Shropshire

Peplow, or Childs Ercall as it was known locally, was located a few miles north of the Wrekin, a prominent landmark in Shropshire. The aircraft there were Wellington Mark IIIs with which I was very familiar. The training procedure was similar to that at Tilstock, in that we trained the pilots to fly the aircraft, and then the other members of the team were added to make up a crew.

After that, as before, we trained the crews in practice bombing and cross-countries day and night. The only occasion there was a variation of routine was when I was with a crew on a night cross-country up the east coast of England. The port engine on our aircraft developed high temperatures and low oil pressure. The engine had to be closed down and this necessitated calling up the emergency services, their presence allowing me to land on the one engine, a tricky manoeuvre at night, at Middleton St George, near Darlington. After an overnight stay, the engine problem was resolved and we were able to continue the exercise, but this time in daylight.

The remainder of the time was routine, so when a volunteer was asked to carry out testing of aircraft leaving the Maintenance Unit, I jumped at the chance. When aircraft came out of the Maintenance Unit they had to be ground-tested and then given a thorough test in the air. On the air tests, I always insisted on taking the riggers and the fitters who had carried out the work on that particular aircraft with me. They were generally happy to come along for the ride, except when I shut down each engine alternately at a certain point in the flight, when they tended to become rather nervous. I reminded them that it was their workmanship that I was testing and that if they had confidence in their own abilities, they had nothing to fear. There is no doubt that some were less encouraged by that thought than others, but that is exactly why I took them with me, and the standard of workmanship increased rapidly.

The Wellington performed well, and one day while out on a test near to the United States Army Air Force base at Atcham, an American P47-D Thunderbolt fighter was climbing slowly after take-off just as I cruised by. The pilot took up a position close to my right wing and flew alongside me. It was time for a little fun with the Yank; I closed down the starboard engine of my Wellington, which slowed me down and so the American pilot also slowed. I then opened the port engine wide. The engine was very responsive and as a result we surged ahead of the Thunderbolt leaving a very surprised American some distance behind us. In due course he caught up with us, and, obviously laughing, waved and sped off. The P47 was quite a fast fighter but it took a little while to work up its speed, which is how I had been able to leave it behind so easily. A little bit of boyish fun in trying times.

One day while taxiing round the perimeter track at Peplow, I noticed a small group of navigators 'swinging the compass' of a Wellington that was standing on a concrete pan inside the perimeter track. Swinging the compass meant moving the aircraft to points north, east, south and west and adjusting the compass to allow for the metal in the aircraft, in order that an accurate reading could be made in the air. One navigator was holding up a marker-board and walking backwards towards me from the parked aircraft, keeping in line with the fuselage, and I suddenly realised he was so engrossed in what he was doing that he was not aware of my approach. I immediately braked and switched off my port engine, but as the port propeller came to a stop, one blade knocked the board out of his hand. He stood there stunned. He had come within an ace of being killed. There had to be an enquiry and, despite my report, the navigators got together, with the result that I received an endorsement for gross carelessness.

While at Peplow, a new flying officer came into the Mess. He commenced training with a crew, but as he neared the end of the course, his skin broke out in a serious rash. His training was put back until his problem cleared up, after which he was teamed up with another crew. Once again towards the end of his course he broke out in a rash. He sat around in the Mess for a while and then disappeared. We heard later that he had resigned his commission and returned to his pre-war career. His name was Michael Rennie, the very good actor who is perhaps best remembered for his starring roles as Klaatu in the 1951 film *The Day the Earth Stood Still*, and later as Harry Lime in the highly memorable 1959 television series *The Third Man*, loosely based upon the 1949 Carol Reed film of the same name with Orson Wells as Lime. A Yorkshire man, Michael was born at Idle, near Bradford in 1909 and sadly died at only sixty-one from an aortic aneurism at his home in Harrogate.

Like Tilstock, and every other training base, there were the inevitable casualties during training:

Date	Aircraft	Accident	Casualties	
			Killed	Injured
3/3/44	Wellington	Engine failure		5
-/3/44	Wellington	Crashed		3
19/5/44	Wellington	Crashed	7	
23/7/44	Wellington	Crashed	6	
27/7/44	Hurricane	Mid-air collision	2	
-/8/44	Wellington	Engine failure	3	3
26/8/44	Wellington	Mid-air collision	11	
Total:			29	11

In spite of everyone's best efforts during the training programme for aircrew, there were many accidents. In total, more than 5,000 aircrew were killed whilst undergoing training through the period of the war.

D-Day had passed, and the Allied forces were on their way into France. I felt I wanted to be involved, so applied for a posting to the Pathfinder Force of Bomber Command. Accordingly, I was posted to train to fly Mosquitoes at 1655 Mosquito Training Unit at Warboys in Cambridgeshire. By now, it was September 1944.

CHAPTER 13
Second Operational Tour – Mosquitoes

The Mosquito in its various forms was a very versatile aircraft. It was used as a fighter, a fighter-bomber, in Coastal Command, in photo reconnaissance, and transporting passengers from neutral Sweden to Britain; but I was to fly the high-level bomber version.

No.1655 Mosquito Training Unit was located at Warboys near Huntingdon. After two hours' training on Mosquitoes I went solo. I then picked up my navigator, Flying Officer Bernard Tubbs, naturally known as 'Tubby' despite being tall and thin. In view of his experience during his first tour of operations on Lancaster bombers, he was appointed Squadron Navigation and Bombing Officer. This behoved us to set a high example to the rest of the squadron in terms of navigation and bombing and to ensure we achieved a high standard of accuracy.

We flew daylight, night bombing and cross-country exercises, becoming well acquainted with the Mosquito B XV1. This was a high-level aircraft designed to fly at 30,000 feet, carried one 4,000lb bomb, and had overload drop tanks for long range, and extensive radar consisting of Gee, H2S, and Loran for accurate pinpointing of targets almost as far away as Berlin. It carried no guns, being dependent on height and speed for survival. It was capable of flying at over 400 mph, about 50 mph faster than a Spitfire, and was an exhilarating aircraft to fly.

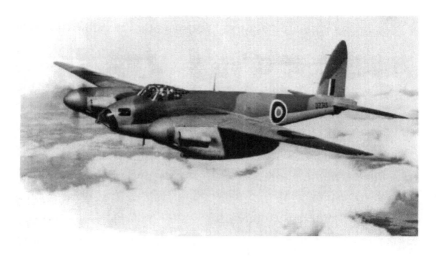

De Havilland Mosquito Mark B XV1

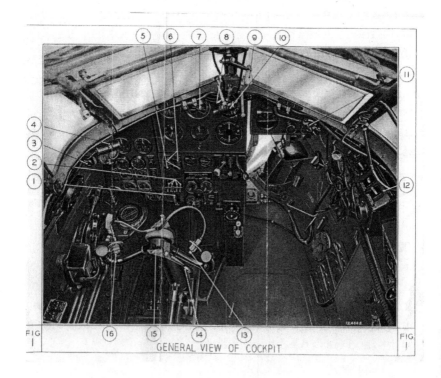

GENERAL VIEW OF COCKPIT

Mosquito cockpit

[courtesy of Crecy Publishing Ltd]

The 4,000lb bomb, known as a 'cookie', was shaped like a long metal barrel, domed at the front, where three proximity fuses were fitted. A conventional bomb, when dropped, exploded on impact and such was its speed of descent that in the milliseconds between impact and detonation it would have dug itself well into the ground before it exploded. Thus, much of the explosive force was absorbed whilst the remainder blew upwards, leaving a large crater in the ground.

The 4,000lb 'cookie' was designed to be different. When loaded into the bomb bay of the aircraft it was fitted with three keys, similar to tuning forks, attached to the three fuses in the nose and which prevented their detonation. The keys had wires attached that were in turn attached to the aircraft. When the bomb left the aircraft, the keys were automatically withdrawn, but it did not become 'live' immediately. Also attached to the fuses were little propellers which unwound themselves as the bomb descended and dropped away, after which the bomb was primed and ready to explode, leaving the bomb 'live'.

As the bomb neared its target, pressure built up between the bomb and the ground, so that at around 15 to 20 feet above the surface, the detonators were activated, and the bomb exploded, causing a tremendous blast effect over a large area.

Loading a 4,000lb 'cookie' [Chas Bowyer]

In our second week of training, we were to fly a daytime cross-country and climb to 30,000 feet above the airfield before setting out. Somewhere above 18,000 feet, I passed out and didn't remember any more until I found we were back at 10,000 feet. On investigation, I discovered that there was a large tear in the flexible tube leading to my oxygen mask, so that I was not receiving any oxygen. Fortunately, Tubby had realised the situation, and reached over to push the control forward and bring us down to a lower altitude, where I recovered.

On one daylight exercise at 33,000 feet on a perfectly clear day travelling up the centre of England, we could see the North Sea on our right and the Irish Sea and Ireland on our left. We felt privileged to be in a position to behold such a spectacle, for in those days only a minority of aircraft were capable of travelling at such high altitude.

After two weeks, we were posted to No.692 [Fellowship of the Bellows] Squadron based at Graveley, near Huntingdon in Cambridgeshire, part of No.8 Group. It was October 1944.

Graveley was also the home of No.35 Pathfinder Lancaster Squadron, and was therefore a busy airfield.

Our 692 Pathfinder Squadron was used in various ways. While the four-engine bomber 'heavies' were bombing their targets, we could be scattered over other parts of Germany to ensure that as many cities as possible were being bombed every night in order to depress German morale, keep them down in their shelters and disrupt war production. Sometimes we would 'mark' a target for the 'heavies'. They would take off for a target but because we were much faster we would leave some time later, catch up with and overtake them, then fly on ahead to arrive at the target sixty seconds before them in order to drop the TI marker flares to identify the point of aim. They would then drop their bomb loads onto the markers.

We were required to fly in all sorts of weather conditions, and on taking off for Germany, it was not unknown for us to enter a cloud base at less than 1,000 feet and not emerge out of it until 22,000 feet.

The only major changes ever made to Mosquitoes were to fit two-stage supercharger engines, add long-range tanks and alter their radar. ML959 features the engine change and, being a Mk.XVI bomber, has a pressure cabin. Used for nine months by No.692 Squadron at Graveley. (de Havilland)

[Courtesy de Havilland]

Our first trip with 692 Squadron was on 29th October to Cologne, a city that had never fully recovered from the 1,000 bomber battering it had received back in 1942. We were part of a force of fifty-nine Mosquitoes attacking the city that night. The defending night fighter force had come a long way, though, in the two years or so since I had been a part of the historic raid, and they were now able to deploy jet fighters which were more than a match for the substantial speed of the Mosquito. However, we didn't lose any aircraft, and although I saw several of these jets, I wasn't sure exactly what they were and fortunately they didn't come close enough for me to see – and I had no intention of going to look for myself! After Cologne, the operations came thick and fast, as by now there was a real belief that the war was entering its final months, although in October 1944 we didn't think that it would be the following May before it was finally over. The forty target cities that made up my second tour were Cologne[1] Hanover[3], Karman[1], Nuremburg[1], Duisburg[2], Karlsruhe[1], Mannheim[1], Erfurt[1], Kassel[1], Bremen[1], Dessau[1], Hamburg[2], Munich[2], Husum[1], Berlin[18], Kiel[2] and Ludwigshafen[1].

Not long after I joined 692 Squadron, I acquired a small Beretta automatic pistol and decided to take it with me on ops. Twenty years later, the Beretta would be the weapon of choice for the fictional James Bond; I was in good company. I knew that if I parachuted to the ground after being shot down over Germany, the civilian population would take their revenge on me as a *'terror flieger'* and I thought that I could at least defend myself with the pistol, if only to save me from being hanged from the nearest lamp post.

Bomber Command dropped 22,580 tons of bombs on the city of Hamburg docks during the war. Two nights after going to Cologne, Halloween brought a trip to Hamburg for me together with forty-eight other Mosquitoes. Hamburg had never recovered from the *Operation Gomorrah* raids in 1943, which created a firestorm and decimated the city, and indeed it didn't do so until the post-war rebuilding took place, but in October

1944, the docks were still operating for the Kriegsmarine. Along with my escape kit and everything else for the mission, I packed my little Beretta. En route to the target, Tubby kept correcting my flying on track but we reached Hamburg on time, bombed accurately from 25,000 feet against heavy flak from the 88mm anti-aircraft batteries, and then started to fly home. We relaxed as much as was possible, bearing in mind we had to keep an eye out for German night fighters.

As we approached the English coast, I decided we should descend safely through the thick cloud over the sea as a safety precaution. As we emerged from the cloud, we could see we were over the sea, but with land showing on both sides. Then the land on the left receded and a quick double check established we were over the English Channel but many miles off course. As we were short of fuel, I made a 'Mayday' call and soon afterwards a searchlight cone appeared on our right; we landed on a small emergency grass airfield at Friston on the top of Beachy Head.

We stayed overnight, refuelled and returned to Graveley next morning, complaining about the compass in the aircraft. I subsequently realised, though, that the considerable compass error was due to my having the Beretta tucked down into my left flying boot adjacent to the compass. The metal of the gun had caused the compass to give a faulty reading. After that, the pistol remained in my locker at the airfield until the end of my tour.

In addition to these Pathfinder missions, we were sent to carry out two daylight raids on Duisburg in the Ruhr on the 29th and 30th November. The target was the tar and benzole plant in the Meiderich district of the city. We were a raid or thirty Mosquitoes flying in three tight formations of ten aircraft each at 25,000 feet with a protective screen of Spitfires overhead. The effect of thirty aircraft each releasing their 4,000lb cookies in quick succession on the city was devastating! Nevertheless, the *Oboe*-leader method had not worked well as two of the formations had failed to link up with their leaders on time and the bombs fell on the docks and to the south. The next day, we did it all again with much more success.

The two back-to-back trips to Duisburg were followed on 1st December by a raid on Karlsruhe, when again we bombed on the TIs from 25,000 feet. All 140 Mosquitoes involved in these three raids returned home safely. Whilst there were losses, and danger still lurked for the unlucky or the unwary, it was now a very different combat zone than I had experienced on my first tour.

The trip to Ludwigshafen was quite eventful for both Tubby and me. It was 5th December 1944, and we were routed via the Thames Estuary, Kent, Calais and then direct to the target. We were to fly at 30,000 feet and mark the target for the 'heavies'. At 5,000 feet, I did a routine check of the engines and found that the oil temperature on both engines was high and the pressures low. I throttled back and levelled out, and after a few minutes, the temperatures returned to just above normal and the pressures returned to just below normal. I opened the throttles again and, after gaining a few more thousand feet, the temperatures rose and the pressures dropped. Again, I levelled out and throttled back, whereupon the temperatures returned to just above normal and the pressures returned to just below normal.

I continued to climb and the performance was repeated until we reached 17,000 feet. By now we were just beyond Calais, and I let the aircraft cruise for ten minutes watching the engines all the while. Everything seemed to have settled down with the temperatures slightly up and the pressures slightly down, so I decided we should go ahead with the operation despite now being late. There was no chance we would be in time to drop TI markers on the target, but at least we could drop our 4,000lb bomb.

Some forty miles from the target, we could see a glow in the sky ahead indicating that the raid was already in progress; it was just then that the port engine gave a cough. The engine temperature was off the high end of the dial and the pressure was showing almost zero. I immediately cut the engine and feathered the propeller to prevent it seizing up and catching fire. Normally, under these circumstances, one opened up the other engine to maintain power and height, but, bearing in mind the state of the starboard engine with its temperatures and pressures, this was not possible, so the starboard engine setting was left as it was. My dilemma was, should I now jettison the bomb or continue to the target? Having come this far, I decided we would continue towards Ludwigshafen, despite the fact that we were losing height and would become an easy target for German gunners when we arrived.

In the end, when we reached Ludwigshafen we were below 5,000 feet and found the city ablaze. We were so late in arriving that the raid was over, the RAF heavy bombers were on their way home and the 'all clear' had been sounded below. We flew over the city, found our target, an aircraft factory, and dropped our bomb. At this, the German defences rushed to their guns once more and poured flak in our direction, but, despite having only one engine, we were able to get away safely.

How we had caught them out and got through was that, although the German radar had picked up our approach to the target, their sound equipment had detected the sound of only one engine, and Allied single-engine aircraft were not seen that far south at night, thus they rather naturally mistook us for one of their own single-engine fighters and did not move to intercept us. We had caught them by surprise but had been very fortunate to do so because it was entirely by luck and not design!

We turned for home, and now, because we had dropped the bomb and used nearly half of our fuel, the aircraft was much lighter and easier to handle, and was in fact now climbing steadily. We slowly managed to reach 18,000 feet, keeping a sharp lookout for German night fighters, and I settled for that height, constantly checking the engine temperatures and pressures. As we crossed the Belgian border, we began to feel some relief at our progress, but then, on checking the engine again, I found the temperature had suddenly shot up and the pressure had dropped. There was no way we were going to get back home. The night was pitch black, with no sign of light on the ground. I throttled back the engine then called 'Mayday' on the emergency radio frequency. I repeated the call three times, but with no success. There was complete silence. We had no choice; we would have to bail out.

Steadily losing height, I gave the order, so Tubby clipped on his parachute and went down to open the lower exit hatch; it was jammed. He came back up and I pulled the lever over my head, at which point the emergency overhead hatch blew away into the night. The aircraft was pressurised and so now air was sucked out of the cockpit to equalise the outside pressure, taking with it maps, charts, pencils, toffee papers and anything else not strapped in. As I reduced the speed of the aircraft to as low as it could possibly go, Tubby stood on his seat facing forward and eased himself up into the slipstream but didn't go. I realised that his foot had caught in the hatch opening, so I stood up, gave his ankle a good pull and he was gone into the night as if he had never been in the aircraft.

Now it was my turn. I had never used a parachute before, but first I had to go through the procedures to shut the aircraft down. I had to switch off the one remaining engine, trim the aircraft into an engineless glide, ease myself out of the top hatch, and then hope that I didn't become entangled with the rudder and elevators at the rear of the aircraft. Whilst I was preparing to do all this, a part of my mind was worrying about how and where I would land in the pitch black that lay below me and whether that landing would be a safe one. My nerves were stretched more tightly than they had been for a long time.

Then, for some reason that I will never know, just before I shut down the starboard engine, I once again put out a 'Mayday' call. Instantly, a voice came back to me through my headset, "Aircraft calling emergency, what is your problem?" "Oh, hell!" I thought, "My navigator has bailed out and now my emergency call is being answered." I reported my problem, requesting immediate landing facilities. There was a quick response: off to my right, six searchlights forming an inverted cone thrust into the sky. I was informed that an emergency airfield was underneath and was asked if I could make it. I would certainly try. I had to keep the starboard engine ticking over because it drove the hydraulic pump which lowered the flaps and undercarriage, but thereby also risked the engine seizing up and catching fire. Additionally, if I got below 5,000 feet and couldn't reach the airfield I would have to bail out anyway before I got too low to be able to use my parachute. I was in touching distance of salvation and yet I could feel the tension building up inside me even more.

I turned the Mosquito towards the cone of light, easing her down on minimum revs, trying desperately to balance the need to keep enough power on to prevent a stall whilst nursing the engine to keep it alive. As soon as I dared, I lowered the undercarriage, despite the drag it would create. Closer and closer the cone of light came, and then at last I could see the aerodrome ahead of me shining through the darkness.

I started my approach, making what in effect was a 'dead stick' landing, that is, there would be no second chance. Then, as I came in over the airfield boundary, I was met by a fearful sight which gripped my stomach at the shock of it. In the light of the searchlights, I could see that the aircraft parked on either side of the runway had large black crosses marked on their wings and fuselages; Luftwaffe aircraft: was this a trap? Had I been duped by the German radio controllers? With a sinking heart, I realised that I was about to become a prisoner of war. My aircraft was not capable of flying any further, and the thought that it was about to be captured as well made things even worse, and there was nothing I could do about it! As all this flashed through my mind, with a sudden fillip of relief and glee, I realised that although they were indeed German aircraft, they had been bulldozed off the runway to keep it clear. My aeroplane touched down and ran to the end of the runway, where I turned off onto the perimeter track and stopped. A light RAF van picked me up and took me to the control tower, where I met the chap in charge of the airfield. He was a flight lieutenant who informed me that I had landed on an emergency forward airfield primarily meant for the use of fighters and tactical aircraft and which had a small maintenance unit for repairing aircraft.

After introducing ourselves and having a coffee, I asked if I could send a signal to Graveley, my home airfield, to tell them where I was. George, the flight lieutenant, said, "No chance, chum. All signal traffic across the Channel is military priority, and I am afraid that does not include you." With that, I was found a bed with the promise they would examine my aircraft the next day if possible.

They were too busy repairing fighters to look at my aircraft the next day, and so that night, George drove me in the little van through the blackout to a bar in the local Belgian village. En route, we passed a couple of horse-drawn wagons, their only illumination being a lit storm lantern hanging underneath the wagon; easy to hit or miss. After we had consumed several lagers, we retired to the loo to take care of nature, and whilst pointing our 'Percies' at the porcelain, I was suddenly shocked to see two women walk past, chatting away merrily. They disappeared into two cubicles at the end of the room. I put my hand down to cover my embarrassment whilst George, completely unabashed, grinned at me and said, "Don't worry, chum, you are in Belgium now... unisex toilets." I was still learning.

The following day, the mechanics drained the oil from the port engine of the Mosquito and found particles of metal, which meant the engine had to have new bearings or be replaced. The starboard engine was very short of oil, but when topped up ran very well. I was asked if I would take off on one engine but, after careful thought, declined. The Mosquito always swung to port on take-off, due to both propellers turning in the same direction, and this was normally countered by opening the port engine in advance of the starboard engine. Without a port engine, braking was the only possibility to keep the aircraft straight but required a longer runway than was available. Additionally, once airborne and losing 'ground effect', the cushion of air between the aircraft and the ground which stabilises the aircraft, the tremendous turning (twisting) moment effect of the 1,650 horsepower engine on just one side of the aircraft, coupled with high wind loading and relatively slow speed, could cause the aircraft to flip over on its back and dive into the ground. I wasn't prepared to commit suicide! George then asked me if I could fly a Wellington. It appeared they had a Wellington in the hangar which they wanted to get back to England, and they could have it made ready for the next day. I naturally agreed to take it, as this was my way of getting home.

That night, George said he would take me to a much better bar in a local town. We went into the bar, which was a half-moon shape with comfortable seating, ordered two lagers and sat against the wall. It was quite a large room, with a large staircase going up from the centre, at the bottom of which sat a huge blousy woman behind the largest National cash register I had ever seen. The room was filled with servicemen, both RAF and Army... and lots of very pretty girls. The latest dance music seemed to be coming from upstairs. I thought how nice it was for our servicemen to be able to go to dances while away from home.

We were drinking our third lager, when a truly beautiful girl of about twenty came over, sat next to me and tapped me on the shoulder. "Hello," she said. "Hello," I replied, and carried on talking to George. Again a tap on the shoulder, "My name is Paulette," she purred. "Hello, Paulette," I said, and went on talking to George. There was another tap on my shoulder. "You not like me?" "Yes, very nice," I answered, and still went on talking.

The next thing I knew, the girl was stroking the inside of my thigh, which I thought was rather forward of her! I looked at George, who was now laughing. Suddenly the penny dropped. This was no dance hall; this was the local official brothel. I said to George, "Look, I am seriously courting a girl back in England and I don't want to get involved here, let's go."

"You can't walk out just like that," George said. "It's only very recently that these people were freed from four years of German occupation, and they now want to show their gratitude by sending you the best girl in the house. You are an RAF flying officer with medal ribbons and to them a hero. If you walk out now you will insult the girl, insult the management, and probably have a pimp stick a knife in you when you get outside." I thought for a moment, then turned to the girl and

said in my atrocious French, "Vous êtes très belle, Paulette."
(You are very beautiful, Paulette). "Merci, monsieur," she
replied. "Malheureusement, je dois vole dans une heure. Je
vous verrais demain soir vers huit heures et demi, oui?"
(Unfortunately I have to fly in an hour. I will see you tomorrow
night at 8.30). "Oui, monsieur," she beamed at me and with
that, we got up, I shook the girl's hand, kissed her on both
cheeks and departed saying, "Au revoir, à bientôt." Of course, I
had no intention of going back the next evening, as I would be
back in England by then. "You cheeky bugger, you talked your
way out of that, but you have spoilt my evening," George
complained bitterly.

The next morning, the Wellington was wheeled out, I ran up
the engines and it seemed perfectly OK. I asked where the
aircraft was to go, and was told it should be flown to Odiham in
Hampshire. My crew for the flight was an aeroplane engine due
for replacement that had been strapped up into the bomb bay,
some spare parts stored inside the aircraft and two airmen who
were cadging a lift home to go on leave. I asked George if he
had any maps, but he hadn't and I had lost mine three nights
before when they were sucked out of the cockpit of the
Mosquito, so it meant flying to Odiham in Hampshire by
guesswork.

I took off, heading in the general direction of the English south
coast, aiming towards Beachy Head, a prominent white cliff
some 500 feet high. I actually struck the English coast at
Eastbourne next to Beachy Head, turned west until I reached
Hayling Island, turned right 90 degrees and headed for Odiham.
I was born and raised ten miles from Odiham, so finding it was
no problem. I landed, taxied up to the control tower, parked,
and went inside. I identified myself and asked to be put through
on the telephone to Graveley. I was put through to my
Commanding Officer.

"Who's that?"

"Trotman here, Sir."

"Trotman. Where are you?"

"I am at Odiham."

"What are you doing there?"

"I have just landed in a Wellington."

"A Wellington? Where is your Mosquito?"

"I had a forced landing and it's in Belgium."

"Why didn't you let me know? You do realise I have advised the Air Ministry that you are missing believed killed in action. What do you want?"

"Will you please send an aircraft to pick me up, Sir?"

"Very well, I'll send an aircraft for you and your navigator."

"Only me. My navigator bailed out two days ago, and I don't know where he is."

"Very well, report back to me when you arrive at Graveley."

"Thank you, Sir."

The CO seemed irritated about having to contact the Air Ministry to advise our safe return. This was the second occasion during my time in the RAF that I had been assumed KIA!

I advised the control tower that an aircraft was coming to pick me up, but I was told I couldn't leave the airfield until I had been cleared by HM Customs officials. It appeared that many RAF aircrew flying from England to the Continent were taking tea, coffee, sugar, bicycle tyres, etc., which were desperately scarce in Europe at the time, and swapping them for crates of wine and champagne. The Government of course, could not permit such individual entrepreneurship unless it had a cut of the profits and decreed that this must stop, hence the necessity for customs clearance. I was told that the customs officers were located at Southampton and that they wouldn't arrive until evening. I had no intention of simply kicking my heels at Odiham all day for their convenience and informed the control staff that if my aircraft came first I would return to Graveley and the customs officers could do what they liked about it. As it happened, my aircraft did come first and I left the customs officers to examine the Wellington I had flown in, at their leisure. I returned to Graveley and made my report.

What happened to Tubby? I was not to find out until some time later, when this was the story he told me. After bailing out somewhere over Belgium, he had landed heavily in a ploughed field, one foot on a ridge and one foot in a furrow, and given himself a black eye. It was pitch dark, so he followed the furrows to the edge of the field, buried his parachute in a ditch and, there being no fences or hedges, clambered up on to a road. He looked up into the sky, found the North Star and proceeded west along the road. After about three miles, he came to a village, and because his eye was giving him a lot of pain he looked for a house or building with a doctor's plaque on it. He was fortunate in having with him a penlight torch, which was standard equipment for navigators in Mosquitoes, where the pilot and navigator sit almost side by side and, because over enemy territory the cockpit lighting was turned right down, a torch was necessary for the navigator to see his maps and charts.

He found a plaque on a house which indicated a Médicin (medical doctor) and banged on the door. After a while, a candle was lit, a window opened and a voice called out, "Oui, qui est là?" (Yes, who's there?). In his best grammar-school French, he told the man who he was, and that he needed attention to his eye. The doctor's answer was an emphatic, "Non, non, non, allez, allez," (No, no, no, go away) and he closed the window. Determined, and in increasing pain, Tubby banged hard on the door again. The window opened once more and the doctor shouted, "Allez, allez, allez-vous en," and at that produced a double-barrelled shotgun which he pointed at Tubby. Whether the doctor had forgotten his Hippocratic Oath or, more likely, feared German reprisals for helping Allied airmen, Tubby cared not; he was clearly not going to help him. So, realising that further entreaties were only likely to result in further injuries, he turned away shouting some good old-fashioned Anglo-Saxon words at the Médicin, the gist of which was to suggest that the doctor's father should have married his mother.

A few more miles down the road, Tubby heard the noise of vehicles coming towards him. During his descent by parachute, he knew that, with the prevailing westerly wind, he would have drifted to the east, but did not know exactly where he was, and realised that these vehicles might be either retreating Germans or advancing Allies. He therefore dropped down into the deep ditch at the side of the road until a number of lorries and half-tracks had lumbered by. He was about to climb out when he realised that the convoy had stopped and he saw, silhouetted against the stars, a stationary vehicle above him. He lay perfectly still. If he approached them and they were Germans, he would probably be shot and left in the ditch.

Then a voice above him said, "Hey, Charlie, gimme a cigarette, will ya." Tubby was out of the ditch in a flash and stepped into the headlights of a Jeep. He heard the command, "Hold it right there, Mac." He saw two automatic pistols pointing at him, so quickly identified himself. "Place your hands on the hood and spread 'em," was the answer. He was searched, put in the front passenger seat of the Jeep, and with a GI sitting behind him holding a pistol in his back, was taken to the nearest American Military Police post.

There, he was questioned and searched again, then transported to an American base camp. He was interrogated by a captain from Intelligence and given medical attention to his eye plus some coffee to drink. In the end, the Intelligence Officer said, "OK, Lieutenant, I'll get in touch with SHAEF (Supreme Headquarters Allied Expeditionary Force) in France. They will contact SHAEF Headquarters in London who will get in touch with your Air Ministry. When you are cleared, we will help you get home. You have the freedom of the Officers' Mess, but don't try to leave the camp. Your uniform looks German, our guards are trigger happy and you might get shot." Tubby was then taken to the Officers' Mess, given a meal of ham, eggs, French fries, canned peaches and ice cream, and found a bed for his stay.

At the end of two days, there was still no news, despite pestering the Intelligence Officer. Then, into the Mess came an American Army Air Force captain wearing wings on his chest. Tubby pounced on him and established he was flying supplies into a local airfield from England. The captain agreed to give Tubby a lift home. The next morning, the two drove out of the camp in an army Jeep, although rather absent-mindedly, Tubby 'forgot' to tell the Intelligence Officer what he was doing! In no time at all, Tubby was in the rear of a DC3 Dakota flying back to England, sitting on crates of fine wine and champagne, none of which, I am sure, were destined to go anywhere near one of His Majesty's Customs officers.

They landed at Eastleigh (now Southampton Airport) and, after receiving a rail pass and money from the American Adjutant, was soon on his way to Waterloo. While in London, he called to see his parents to tell them he was safe and sound, then returned to Graveley to make his report. I was heartily pleased to see him.

What was the cause of the problem with the aircraft? Because the Mosquito flew at 30,000 feet where the temperature could be as low as -50°C, it was necessary to blank off the oil radiators to some extent to prevent freezing of the oil. The oil radiators were located in the leading edges of the wings between the engines and the fuselage, and the amount of blanking required depended on the variation in temperature. At the end of November, the temperature on the ground had been -3°C, but within a few days had changed to +6°C. Since the temperature at altitude is related to the temperature on the ground, on the night we left for Ludwigshafen the radiator blanking should have been reduced, but our aircraft-fitter had forgotten to do it.

The result was that the engines overheated, and the aeroplane and its crew failed to return. The fitter confessed to his error and was arrested pending a court martial. However, since we had returned after a few days and later fetched the aircraft back from Belgium, we persuaded the CO to reduce the charge against the fitter to twenty-eight days confined to camp.

It was as a result of this adventure that I was recommended for my first Distinguished Flying Cross [DFC]. When it came through on 2nd January 1945, I also received a congratulatory Postagram from Air Chief Marshal AT Harris, the Commander-in-Chief of Bomber Command. For a flying officer to receive a personal message from the most senior officer in the Command was a particularly proud moment for me and not one that I could ever have dreamed of back in the summer of 1940 when I first joined the RAF. My award was published in the *London Gazette* on 13th February 1945.

CHAPTER 14
The beginning of the end

1944 had been particularly noted for the D-Day invasion of Europe by the Allies on 6th June. Shortly afterwards, the Germans began bombarding London with flying 'buzz' bombs, the V1, followed in September by the use of V2 rockets, the world's first long-range ballistic missile. In the Far East, June also saw advances against the Japanese in occupied Burma.

As is so often the case in life, when one is granted joy and happiness, there is a price to be paid. For me, it was that the news of my DFC was tinged with the sadness at the loss a good friend the day before during a daylight raid whilst he was trying to 'throw' a delayed-action bomb into the mouth of a tunnel during the Ardennes counter-offensive, better known as the Battle of the Bulge.

By the winter of 1944, the Allied advance towards Germany from the west had largely ground to a halt, more or less along the German border. Operation Market Garden, the plan to capture the Rhine bridges, including the one at Arnhem, the bridge too far, had, despite the immense courage and fortitude of the paratroopers involved, failed to make the decisive breakthrough, and a long winter lay ahead.

The Germans realised that the Allied supply lines were stretched beyond capacity, whilst their own were now much shorter following their retreat after the D-Day invasion. There was one last chance left to Hitler for a counter-attack through the Ardennes forest, an area held by relatively few American troops.

On 16th December, the Germans launched their offensive along an eighty-mile front and caught the Allies by surprise. The weather was not good and neither the RAF nor the USAAF could give the ground troops any air cover for some days.

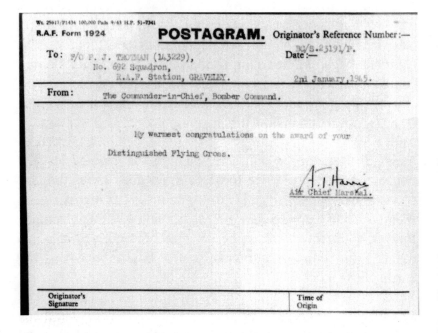

My DFC congratulatory telegram from Air Chief Marshal Harris

The Germans, with their backs to the Fatherland, were receiving their supplies via rail links. As we had seen in the battle for the Arnhem bridge, the Germans, with characteristic efficiency, were very good at moving large quantities of men and equipment by rail over large distances in a short space of time. We had learned that lesson the hard way at Arnhem; now we were going to benefit from it. Loaded with supplies, the trains had to pass through a series of tunnels in the hills and wooded Eifel area between the Ardennes and the Rhine, not far from Cologne.

On 1st January, the Squadron was quickly briefed with the plan of attack: the Mosquitoes were to fly down the railway cuttings leading to these tunnels in order to 'throw' delayed-action bombs into the tunnel mouths. These were timed to explode after all the aircraft were safely clear of the scene, causing the tunnels to collapse. Straightforward enough in principle but by no means an easy feat to achieve. Even though the tunnels were fairly lightly manned by older troops, they were protected by 20mm ack-ack guns, which were lethal to low-flying aircraft, and so surprise was essential to allow each Mosquito to get in, release its bomb and get out again. This was an extremely hazardous technique for which the chosen crews had not had chance to practise, needing careful and accurate flying. Fourteen tunnels were attacked in this way on that New Year's day 1945 by seventeen aircraft, with the loss of just one: George Nairn's Mosquito was last seen going down with one engine in flames. I was not on the mission that day but I grieved the loss of another good friend.

During our Pathfinder tour, there were inevitably a few incidents where good luck determined that I should survive. Taking off on a trip to Germany, I was climbing away from the airfield when, at 2,000 feet, the port engine coughed, spluttered and lost power. The Mosquito could not maintain height on one engine at this critical point with full petrol tanks, overload drop petrol tanks, a 4,000lb bomb and full radar equipment. We were overloaded well above the AUW and, unless I fixed the problem immediately, the aircraft would crash and explode. With frantic urgency, I thrust the mixture and throttle levers on the port engine back and forth. Suddenly, the engine burst back into life, giving me full power. Luckily, I had been able to clear the blockage in the fuel system, but even so, in those few seconds we had dropped below 1,000 feet before we were able to climb away. The relief was tremendous. Death had been very close, and I thanked God that I had been able to take the right emergency action because there would have been no second chance. I was soaked in perspiration. I didn't have to look at Tubby to see how he was; I knew he had started to breathe again.

On another occasion, on taking off from the runway, I opened the port engine in advance of the starboard engine in the normal way to prevent the aircraft swinging to the left but, despite every effort, the aircraft continued to swing to the left. Down each side of the runway were long metal troughs supported on steel posts eighteen inches high, which, when necessary, carried petrol which was ignited and gave off a tremendous heat to dispel fog, a system known by the acronym FIDO, standing for Fog Investigation and Dispersal Operation or Fog Intense Dispersal Of. My aircraft now careered towards the troughs, which fortunately were not lit, and without much speed but with use of the ailerons and control column, I managed to hop over the troughs onto the grass beside the runway. By sheer good fortune, the undercarriage stood up to the strain; if it had collapsed, the aircraft would have dropped on to its belly with the possibility of the 4,000lb bomb exploding. Another dice with death – and another big sigh of relief! Take-off was one of the most dangerous parts of every mission and too many crews came to grief in those few moments.

One moonlit night over western Germany returning from a raid, I glanced over to my right and saw, 300 feet below and ahead of me, a Messerschmitt 110 night fighter. It was converging on my path and passing from right to left underneath me. It was in a perfect position for me to attack and shoot it down, but fortunately for the three German airmen aboard, I had no guns. I peeled off to the right and lost sight of him. The 110s and Ju88s were the scourge of our heavy bombers and I would have happily shot it down. In the event, the crew lived to attack our airmen again.

One of the strategies of Bomber Command, which the Mosquito in particular aided to great effect, was to attack as many targets as possible on the same night. This spread the disruption far and wide, ensured that the enemy was always at full defensive stretch, gave little relief to the defenders and undermined civilian morale. For the German people, the bombing must have seemed relentless, for whilst the RAF attacked by night, the USAAF followed on and bombed by day. In the twenty-four hours of the 15th March, some fifteen different German cities were attacked by various aircraft from different Groups, with Berlin being targeted twice.

For us that night, it was Berlin yet again at the end of the piece of red tape on the operations map. The pace of operations remained unrelenting as we tried to pile on the pressure to break the remnants of Nazi resolve and hasten the end of the war. By now, the outcome was not really in doubt, but whether it would be in a week, a month or another year, who could tell? When we arrived over the city, a haze hung like an unwashed net curtain, but I could see the target and bombed it accurately. Suddenly, we were illuminated by German searchlights, caught by the pale blue radar-controlled light and then coned by all the others. My stomach tightened; I hadn't experienced this since laying mines in the U-boat lanes of Saint-Nazaire. I brought the aircraft round in a tight turn to the left and, looking back, realised that we had been leaving a vapour trail behind us which had been picked up by the Germans.

However, despite being caught in this cone of brilliant white light, there was no flak coming up at us, and that meant only one thing – there was a German night fighter in the immediate vicinity! At that time we had become aware that the Luftwaffe had started to use the Me252 Schwalbe (Swallow) jet fighter armed with four 30mm cannon; this was a formidable adversary. Immediate evasive action was necessary! I put the aircraft nose down, quickly gathering speed and, with the aid of a high westerly wind, headed eastwards towards the Russian area, gaining a ground speed of well over 400 mph and quickly leaving the searchlights behind. I then turned to the north, and then the west and headed for home, with a big sigh of relief, thankful to have escaped attack. I experienced that same prickly feeling I had had down the back of my neck way back in 1942 when flying an Airspeed Oxford on night exercises whilst being stalked by an enemy night fighter.

Although I had used all my speed on that occasion to get away from the searchlights and fighters protecting Berlin, it was not our fastest return trip from Berlin. On another occasion, towards the end of the war, I put the nose of the Mosquito down slightly and pushed the throttles open wide. There was relatively little headwind on that occasion and we travelled from Berlin to the English coast, a distance of nearly 500 miles, in just over an hour, which was an extraordinary performance for an aircraft at the time.

In the circuit at Graveley on the downwind leg, there was a hill with a flat top on which the Forestry Commission had grown some young fir trees. One night, one of our crews returned from operations and forgot to adjust his altimeter. He was therefore flying lower than his altimeter indicated, and on the downwind leg prior to landing, he flew his aircraft straight into the trees on the plateau. As the Mosquito ploughed a furrow through the young fir trees, it shed its engines and then its wings. When the fuselage finally came to rest, the two crewmen were left sitting at the controls of a flightless aircraft unharmed but very embarrassed.

As had been the case with my previous squadron, we did manage to get short breaks between operations and we took every opportunity to get away from the station. One night, three of us went to Cambridge in a colleague's car, and after a few drinks heard that there was a nurses' dance being held at the main hospital in the town. We went to the dance, but found the overwhelming presence of protective doctors and the matron detracted from the atmosphere. We therefore took the lift to the basement, where we found the janitor, and, after a chat, found a wheelchair. With one chap sitting in the wheelchair and two pushing him, we went through the hospital floor by floor visiting the patients and wishing them well. A problem only arose when we got to the maternity unit and went round kissing all the mothers and babies. The mothers certainly thought it was great fun, but the babies seemed to object, which roused the matron and sisters, who promptly ejected us from the hospital.

At the airfield, there was a compound in which cars belonging to pilots and navigators who had gone missing or been killed were kept. Since my old Ford had now given up the ghost, I needed another car, so I wrote a tactful letter to a pilot's widow asking if she wished to have her husband's car returned to her, and making it clear that if she did not, I would be interested in buying it. She wrote a very nice letter back saying she would be happy to sell me the car, which I bought at the market value. After some work, it proved very reliable. Later, when the squadron disbanded and I had had a lot of use out of the vehicle, I sold it to my commanding officer at a useful profit, enabling me to upgrade to an even better car.

The approaching defeat of the enemy was something that we sensed on operations rather than anything that was reported on the BBC news or in the papers. Bomber Command maintained the pressure on German targets but it had become unusual to see a night fighter. For the most part, the Luftwaffe was a spent force; there were few aircraft left for its pilots to fly and little or no aviation fuel available to its squadrons. There is no doubt about the commitment of those pilots who did get into the air, but Bomber Command's losses, once counted in double figures night after night, were now in single figures, and sometimes several days would go by without any at all.

On 19th April, Tubby and I took off for Berlin yet again. We had been there the previous night but had been met with only light flak. This would be our eighteenth and final mission to the German capital and on this night there was no flak at all; the defences had effectively collapsed. All seventy-six Mosquitoes returned safely.

The next night, another seventy-six Mosquitoes made six separate attacks upon the city. In a strange way, and in retrospect, having been so many times before, I was a little disappointed not to have gone on this operation because it was the RAF's final raid of the war on Berlin. It would have been nice to have dropped the last bomb, but that honour fell to the crew of Mosquito Mk XVI ML929 of 109 Squadron. At 02.14 on 21st April 1945, FO AC Austin and FO P Moorhead dropped four 500lb bombs on the wreckage of the city below them. They, and all the other aircraft out that night, returned safely, although 3 Group had lost a Lancaster earlier on the 20th during a daylight raid against the oil plant at Regensburg.

In the evening light of 25th April, 107 Lancasters and 12 Mosquitoes took off to attack the oil refinery at Tonsberg in southern Norway. This was the last raid of the war by heavy bombers and was very successful, causing considerable damage to the refinery. All but one of the 119 aircraft returned. The one which didn't was a Lancaster of 463 Squadron, the last one of more than 3,300 Lancasters lost during the war. The bomber crash-landed in Sweden where all of FO Cox's crew survived and were interred until the end of the war, a fortnight later.

On 26th April, Operation Exodus, the rapid repatriation of Allied POWs, began. By VE Day, more than 75,000 prisoners had been brought home by the RAF. That night, our target was Husum aerodrome, where we bombed from 7,000 feet, severely damaged the hangars and runways and put the airfield out of use.

Three days later saw the start of Operation Manna, where for the next nine days, Lancasters of 1, 3 and 8 Group made 2,835 flights to drop 6,672 tons of food to the starving Dutch population; just part of the reason why, even to this day, the Dutch people remain so friendly to the British.

I may not have dropped the last bombs on Berlin, but I did fly on the last two operational missions of the war carried out by Bomber Command. After the Husum airfield raid, the next and very last mission was to Kiel on Wednesday 2nd May 1945. Hitler had committed suicide on 30th April and there was a general feeling amongst the Command's squadrons that our war in Europe was over; the job had been done, we had prevailed and the Nazi war machine had been defeated: but not quite.

A substantial number of German troops had gathered in Kiel and it was thought that the plan was to move them across the Baltic to Norway, from where the war would be continued. And so the last operation was ordered. It fell to 8 and 100 Group squadrons to prevent this rear-guard action. The first wave of fifty-three Mosquitoes attacked airfields around Kiel with bombs and napalm. It was here, within a week of peace in Europe, that the first of the night's tragedies for the Command occurred, when the aircraft of FO R Catterall, DFC and Flt Sgt DJ Beale was lost, killing both airmen.

Later in the night, we went in in two raids, an hour apart, and attacked the port from 18,000 feet. There were no defences and we bombed the city on the TIs using *Oboe* through the 8/10 cloud cover. All 126 Mosquitoes returned home safely, and now our war in Europe really was over. However, the second tragedy of the night was unfolding when two Halifaxes of 199 Squadron collided on their bombing run. Unusually, each Halifax had a crew of eight that night, and thirteen of them would not see VE Day. They were the last Bomber Command casualties during hostilities of the war in Europe and were mainly second-tour men, twelve from Britain and one from the Irish Republic.

The deaths of all 55,573 young men from Bomber Command lost during the Second World War are deeply felt, but perhaps these fifteen, all of whom are buried in the Kiel War Cemetery, are particularly felt because they came so close to the end and on the very last raid when they had already survived so much.

The German troops who had gathered in Kiel all left next morning and it was declared an open and undefended city. Thirty-six hours later, British and Canadian troops quietly occupied the city.

When VE Day came on 8th May, we celebrated along with the rest of the nation. Two weeks later, I flew with Tubby and our rigger and fitter ground staff on a 'Cook's Tour' of Germany, flying at around 3,000 feet. Our route was the Ruhr, Hamm, Hanover, Bremen, Osnabruck and back to Graveley in just less than four hours. We were all astonished at the sight of the devastated German cities, which were mainly just piles of rubble and streets of ruined buildings, many with only a couple of walls standing.

The end of the war in Europe also brought my second tour of operations to an end. I had completed another forty missions, bringing my total of operations against the enemy to seventy. I had faced intense flak, searchlights and night fighters; I had attacked targets over land and sea; I had laid mines at less than 100 feet in the face of determined defenders and dropped bombs from 25,000 feet; I had suffered engine failure, escaped three crashes and come within a whisker of several others; I had been incredibly lucky to survive. The end of this tour also brought another very proud moment for me when, as a result of completing seventy operations successfully and contributing to the downfall of Berlin late in the war, I was awarded a Bar to my DFC. My award was published in the *London Gazette* on 26th October 1945.

Graveley Memorial

692 Squadron

After this, we were told that we were to be posted to the Far East to fight the Japanese. It was decided, however, that before we could go, our Mosquitoes were to be 'tropicalised' to cope with the heat, humidity and termites in the region. Fortunately for us, this project was considerably delayed and eventually abandoned. Then, on 6th August, the Americans dropped an atomic bomb on Hiroshima followed by another one on Nagasaki three days later. Stunned by the irresistible destructive power of these weapons, the Japanese surrendered on the 15th.

VJ Day brought an end to the war and with it more celebrations; shortly after this, the Squadron was disbanded. I was offered a position ferrying Mosquitoes from Gander in Newfoundland to Prestwick in Scotland via Greenland and Iceland. I learned, however, that there was considerable risk in this venture as the weather in both Greenland and Iceland could 'close down' with fog and mist at very short notice, leaving aircraft in the air with nowhere to land. I felt that this was a very dangerous occupation, and so declined the posting. I had been fortunate enough to survive two operational tours and I didn't want to push my luck.

Squadron and Log Book records for my second Tour of Operations

692 Squadron PFF

Date	Aircraft	Target	Remarks
29.10.44	Mosquito XVI	Cologne	Successful raid. Heavy flak. Fires seen from previous night raid. Jet night fighters seen.
31.10.44	Mosquito XVI	Hamburg	Vis clear. Target hit. Heavy flak. Bombed from 25k feet. Night fighters seen [1 a/c lost]
10.11.44	Mosquito XVI	Hanover	Vis clear. Moderate flak. Bombed from 25k feet with 4k lb bomb. No night fighters seen.
11.11.44	Mosquito XVI	Karman	Cloud 10/10. Moderate flak. Bombed on dead reckoning & Gee radar. 1 a/c aborted

21.11.44	Mosquito XVI	Hanover	Vis clear. Heavy flak. Dropped TIs & bombed.
24.11.44	Mosquito XVI	Berlin	Cloud 10/10. Bombed on TIs from 25k feet. Little flak
25.11.44	Mosquito XVI	Nuremburg	Cloud 5/10 @ 10k feet. Moderate flak. Dropped & bombed on TIs from 27k feet. Huge fires seen.
27.11.44	Mosquito XVI	Hanover	Abandoned trip to Berlin > fuel problems. Bombed Hanover as alternative. Little flak. Sky clear.
29.11.44	Mosquito XVI	Duisburg	1st daylight raid by Mosquitoes. Tight formation @ 25k feet. 4k lb bomb dropped visually. Spitfire escort. Good vis. Light flak.
30.11.44	Mosquito XVI	Duisburg	2nd daylight raid. 8 a/c dropped 8 x 4k lb bombs in quick succession in small area. Spitfire escort.

			Light flak.
01.12.44	Mosquito XVI	Karlsruhe	Cloud 9/10. Light flak. Bombed on TIs from 25k feet. Large fires seen through gap in clouds.
05.12.44	Mosquito XVI	Ludwigshafen	Cloud 5/10. Engines overheated. 1 failed en route. Continued to target losing height. Bombed from 5k feet. 2 large explosions.
05.02.45	Mosquito XVI	Berlin	Cloud 10/10. Light flak. Dropped & bombed on TIs. 1 a/c landed @ Coltishall. 2 a/c bombed secondary target.
18.02.45	Mosquito XVI	Mannheim	Cloud 10/10. Bombed on TIs & radar. Moderate flak. [1 a/c lost]
21.02.45	Mosquito XVI	Berlin	Vis clear. Moderate flak. Accurate bombing on target with TIs. 1 a/c bombed Osnabrück > fuel problems. 1 a/c

			returned.
23.02.45	Mosquito XVI	Berlin	Cloud 10/10. Light flak. Bombed on TIs & radar. [1 a/c lost]
25.02.45	Mosquito XVI	Erfurt	Patchy cloud. Light flak. Bombed on TIs from 10k feet. Large fires noted in centre of town.
27.02.45	Mosquito XVI	Berlin	Cloud 10/10. Light flak. Bombed on TIs & radar. Flares dropped from enemy fighters.
28.02.45	Mosquito XVI	Berlin	High thin cloud. Moderate flak. Target clear. Good concentration bombing on target. Large blue flash seen on ground.
02.03.45	Mosquito XVI	Kassel	Cloud 10/10. Moderate flak. Bombed on TIs & radar from 25k feet. Glow of fires through cloud.
05.03.45	Mosquito	Berlin	Ground haze. Moderate flak. Bombed from 25k

	XVI		feet but TIs scattered.
09.03.45	Mosquito XVI	Berlin	Cloud 9/10. Light flak. 100 Mosquitoes bombed on TIs from 25k feet. Huge explosion seen.
12.03.45	Mosquito XVI	Berlin	Cloud 7/10. Moderate flak. Bombed on TIs. Some fires seen.
13.03.45	Mosquito XVI	Bremen	Cloud 10/10. Moderate flak. Bombed on TIs & radar. Large yellowish explosion seen.
15.03.45	Mosquito XVI	Berlin	Ground haze. Target seen visually & hit. Own a/c coned by 12 searchlights picking up my con trail. Dived to east @ high speed.
16.03.45	Mosquito XVI	Berlin	Cloud 6/10. Light flak. Bombed Osnabrück > generator fault.
21.03.45	Mosquito XVI	Berlin	Vis clear. Heavy flak. Target bombed visually. Many searchlights.

			Many fires seen. 1 a/c returned to Brussels > engine fault.
23.03.45	Mosquito XVI	Berlin	Vis clear. Heavy flak. Target bombed visually. Bombing concentrated. Many searchlights. 1 a/c hit badly by flak.
26.03.45	Mosquito XVI	Berlin	Low cloud & haze. Some flak. Bombed on TIs & radar. Few searchlights. 1 a/c returned to Swannington > fuel shortage.
08.04.45	Mosquito XVI	Dessau	Cloud 4/10. No flak. Adverse winds. Poor marking. Difficulty in identifying target. Some fires seen.
10.04.45	Mosquito XVI	Berlin	Cloud 5/10. Some flak & searchlights. Bombed on TIs & radar. [1 a/c lost].
12.04.45	Mosquito XVI	Berlin	Vis clear. Slight haze. Moderate flak & searchlights. Target

			bombed visually.
13.04.45	Mosquito XVI	Hamburg	Cloud 10/10. Light flak. Bombed on TIs & radar. Fire glow below cloud.
16.04.45	Mosquito XVI	Munich	Cloud 2/10. Moderate flak. Target bombed visually. Fires seen. 1 a/c returned to Brussels > engine fault.
18.04.45	Mosquito XVI	Berlin	Cloud 4/10. Light flak. Dropped TIs & bombed. Heavy explosions seen.
19.04.45	Mosquito XVI	Berlin	Vis good. Some haze. No flak. Bombed on TIs. Some fires seen.
23.04.45	Mosquito XVI	Kiel	Cloud 7/10. Moderate flak. Fires seen & many explosions.
24.04.45	Mosquito XVI	Munich	Vis good. Light flak. Visual bombing on rail sidings & phasing transformer station from 13k feet.

26.04.45	Mosquito XVI	Husum Airfield	Cloud 7/10. No flak. Bombed from 7k feet. Runways & hangars severely damaged.
02.05.45	Mosquito XVI	Kiel	Cloud 8/10. No opposition. Bombed on TIs & radar from 8k feet.
08.05.45	-	-	VE Day
08.05.45	Mosquito XVI	-	Ruhr, Hamm, Hanover, Bremen, Osnabrück. Took ground crew to see devastated German cities.

CHAPTER 15
After VJ Day

I decided to take a course at the Central Navigation School at Shawbury in Shropshire to obtain a navigation qualification, which I felt would be of value if I ever decided to go into civil aviation. This course was attended by highly qualified navigators, the only exceptions being another pilot and myself, and within two weeks, it was evident to both of us that we were out of our depth, so we left the course; the remaining members went on to navigate around the world.

I was then posted to Upper Heyford, where we trained new intakes to fly Airspeed Oxfords and Mosquitoes. Amongst this intake were members of the newly formed French Air Force who spoke no English. After they were qualified to fly Oxfords, our job was to teach them to fly Mosquitoes. Even with our basic knowledge of French, supplemented with reading aloud from French/English dictionaries, this was an impossible task. We could not find a dictionary that contained advanced flying terms and words, so we had to use a form of 'Franglais', a mixture of French and English. A number of crashes ensued when the Frenchmen were left to their own devices. Finally, common sense prevailed, and it was decided we should teach English-speaking Frenchmen to fly our aircraft, and then they would in turn teach their countrymen.

While I was at Upper Heyford, a colleague named Jimmy received an invitation to an engagement party at Edgbaston in Birmingham. Jimmy accepted and asked me and another chap to join him. It transpired that the girl getting engaged was an old flame of Jimmy's, with whom he had lost touch. We arrived at a large house, were welcomed by the girl's parents, and enjoyed the hospitality of the food and drinks. We noticed that Jimmy and the girl were regarding each other with very fond looks, and more. Sometime later, the newly engaged young man asked us if we had seen either Jimmy or his fiancée. We knew exactly what those 'fond looks' had led to and why they had both disappeared. It fell to us to keep the young man talking and drinking until eventually Jimmy and the girl reappeared looking like the cats that had very definitely had the cream. Not wanting to be complicit in the inevitable unseemly outcome if Jimmy and this girl spent any more time in each other's company, we quickly said our goodbyes to her parents and hustled Jimmy out of the house and back to the airfield before the situation got out of hand. Whether the young man ever got to marry his fiancée, I didn't hear.

In March 1946, I was posted to RAF Cottesmore and it was here that my future was settled. I had applied for a permanent commission in the Air Force and had been granted extended service as a prelude. There were two factors that affected my thoughts about staying in the RAF. First, the attitude and philosophy had changed as, with the end of the war, flying was no longer the be-all and end-all of policy. During the war, every effort was made to keep aircraft and crews in the air. In peacetime, with the post-war Attlee Government drastically reducing defence costs, flying was reduced to a minimum and efforts were made to keep aircrews occupied on ground duties.

At the same time that I was at Cottesmore, there were two squadron leaders who had not become reconciled to the fact that the war was over. In the Officers' Mess, they acted like hooligans, playing rugby with cushions and chairs, drinking heavily, and making their presence felt by being generally obnoxious, but because of their rank, little was done about it. Their favourite prank was to go round the officers' sleeping quarters in the early hours of the morning tipping people out of bed. They did this to me once, but the second time they tried to do it, I heard them coming. As one of the drunken squadron leaders burst into my room, I grabbed hold of him, pinned him up against the wall, closed the door and told him that if he ever burst into my room again I would give him a good hiding. I then threw him out of the door into the passage, where he fell on the floor. I knew that as a mere flight lieutenant I had overstepped the mark and, knowing this particular person, that my life in future would be made very difficult. I sat down there and then and wrote a letter to the Commanding Officer telling him that I had decided to withdraw my application for a permanent commission.

Later that day, I was told to report to the Commanding Officer, an elderly group captain who had seen a lot of service and was close to retirement. I stood to attention in front of him as, throwing my letter towards me across his desk, he asked me why I had changed my mind about staying in the RAF. His manner was pompous; I was not asked to stand at ease or sit down and this lack of courtesy made me angry. I told him I wasn't prepared to stay in the RAF alongside drunken brawling squadron leaders, and if this was typical of the post-war RAF, I wanted no part of it. He never appeared in the Mess, except on formal occasions and so I also told him he should have made his presence felt in the Mess to prevent that sort of thing happening.

I had made my decision and had nothing to lose, so I spoke my views very bluntly and it was apparent the group captain had never been spoken to like that before. He became red in the face, and told me he could court martial me for insubordination. I told him he had no case as I had plenty of witnesses, confirmed that I wished to leave the RAF as soon as possible, gave a smart salute, turned about and marched out of the room. I was de-mobilised very shortly after. I heard later that the group captain visited the Mess unexpectedly one night, as a result of which the two squadron leaders were separately posted elsewhere.

Back in my home village of Bentley, I had a plan to open a petrol station, garage, café and motel located between the existing main road and the proposed new bypass, but I found after much effort that there were too many obstacles in obtaining land, planning permission, financial support, and overcoming local opposition. I therefore moved north to Shropshire, where I started work with Hoover servicing vacuum cleaners, which I thought would give me time to look for a position more to my liking. In the event, I stayed with Hoover for over 30 years.

My divorce from Audrey came through in early 1946, and in December I remarried. My new wife Joyce was totally against me flying again. She took the view that after spending 5½ years in the RAF, clocking up nearly 2,000 hours of flying, completing 70 operations and walking away from 3 crashes, enough was enough!

Joyce

I had met Joyce whilst stationed in Shropshire. Her father had a smallholding and her mother kept a village store and café. We struck up a rapport which slowly blossomed, and we maintained contact while she was called up and served in the ATS in London and Winchester. Immediately after the war she worked as a secretary to a local company director.

I concentrated on my career with Hoover, progressing fairly rapidly and was one of the first managers to introduce dealer incentives when products became more plentiful after the post-war shortages. Life with Hoover meant having to move home fairly frequently to different parts of the country, starting in Shropshire, then Carlisle, Birmingham, Bristol, Cheshire, and London. I also worked in the USA and Canada, and regularly went in and out of Europe. Whatever flying I did, to America, Canada and Europe, both on business trips and on holiday, was purely as a passenger in commercial aircraft.

Joyce coped well with the changes and upheavals, and made many new friends as we progressed. Our two boys attended no fewer than seven different schools, which proved difficult for them due to different standards of teaching in each school, but they managed well. Michael obtained O and A levels, then attended a local college, gaining an HND in Business Studies. He then obtained qualifications as a Member of the Institute of Management and Marketing and, after working in various companies, subsequently set up a consultancy business, employing some 40 people. Peter, the younger of the two, was very music-orientated, playing in groups around the country: he was also a talented artist, and later became very adept with computers.

Michael [top] and Peter

When I retired from Hoover, Joyce and I moved to Whitchurch in Shropshire, where we bought a piece of land and built a bungalow to our own design. We moved into it in 1983.

Pear Tree Lane

We lived there happily for ten years until, in 1993, Joyce was diagnosed as having non-Hodgkin lymphoma disease. There followed two periods of chemotherapy over the next two years, followed by a remission, and then it recurred in 2000. She appeared to be more concerned at losing her hair than with the disease itself, but retained a good sense of humour throughout. Despite further chemotherapy and radiotherapy, and the hard work done by the consultant, she died at home with her family around her three days before Christmas Day in 2002. It was a battle we had fought together, but finally lost.

I had never in my life thought that Joyce would pre-decease me, so even though we knew the inevitable would happen, it still came as a blow and a shock. I stayed on in the bungalow, and then one month after Joyce's death, my telephone rang at 2 o'clock in the morning. It was the voice of my sister-in-law Olga saying in a quavering tone, "He's gone. Reg is dead." I scrambled into some clothes and drove the five miles to their home. An ambulance crew was there, and they confirmed the death and then waited for the doctor and the police. After that, the local funeral directors called and took away the body. I comforted and helped my sister-in-law through the initial crisis. They had no children of their own. It had not been a good end to one year or start to the next.

Olwen

Chapter 16
A new life

Gradually, my life began to establish a pattern. Attending refresher courses in French and German, I bought myself a new computer and attended computer courses. I stayed with friends in Normandy for a week, stayed with my son Michael in Beaconsfield whilst visiting Kew records to research my old squadron activities, and stayed with friends in Solihull.

As a result of wartime air crashes, twice falling off ladders, and acting as a carer to my late wife, my back was giving me considerable pain. After a personal recommendation, I asked a semi-retired physiotherapist who had previously been in charge of the Physiotherapy Department at Whitchurch Hospital if she would give me some treatment. Olwen, who was widowed, was very good at her profession and soon had me much improved after only three treatments. Subsequently, I foolishly strained my back and had to go to her for more healing. Typically, Olwen would not accept any money for her ministrations.

In our conversations whilst she was treating me, I established that her late husband, a farmer, had died of cancer in 1999. She had continued working with some 30 cattle and calves, 200 pigs, and a miscellany of other animals. She was also doing part-time physiotherapy, was President of the local Bowling Club, was a Parish Councillor, was on the Cemetery Committee, and was involved with the local Women's Institute. Her farm property was crammed with her own and her late husband's furniture, her late parents-in-law's furniture, and her own mother's furniture. One of her four sons, who worked locally, lived at the farm with her, giving her some help. The place needed some TLC.

In view of her kindness to me in sorting out my back problem, I told her I would call at her home one day a week, and help her sort out the chaos and regain some sort of order. Slowly, over quite a period, the house came into shape, and in the course of this activity we became good friends. She introduced me to the husband of a friend of hers who was a prominent member of the Shropshire Flying Club. A club member, John Wojka, son of Adam Wojka, a Battle of Britain pilot, invited me to go flying with him, and I was encouraged to take over the controls. I discovered to my surprise and delight that it was like riding a bicycle, you never forget. Even after a gap of over 50 years, I had not lost the ability to handle an aircraft. Accordingly, I joined the Flying Club, took a course requiring fifty hours of flying and took seven exams covering all aspects of flying, including navigation, radio, meteorology, etc., needing to get 80% pass marks in all subjects. This all took quite a while, because I was recovering from a broken pelvis at the time.

After my first solo flight, I was confronted, to my great surprise, by the local press and Midland Television cameras. It reminded me of my very first solo flight back in 1940 when I had been mentioned in the *News Chronicle*.

Me, flying again
[courtesy of the Shropshire Star]

The final flying test had to be taken with the Chief Flying Instructor, but because of poor weather, there was going to be a five-week wait for the test. Rather than wait, Olwen and I flew with Ryanair down to Jerez in Spain, where I was able to take my test immediately under warm blue skies with Keith Walker, who had been my instructor all along and was now my examiner. I was very grateful to Keith for all he had done because now I had a private pilot's licence at the age of 85!

As a bonus, Keith and I hired an aeroplane and flew with our wives, from Jerez, off the southern coast of Spain down the Straits between North Africa and Spain, round Gibraltar and back via Malaga and the mountains of Southern Spain.

Olwen encouraged me to join and get involved with the Royal Air Force Association, Probus, the Aircrew Association, and to become a committee member of a supper club. She also encouraged me to regain contact with Sonia, my daughter from my first marriage, and this led to an emotional meeting. Sonia had qualified as a dentist, and was now a Professor of Dentistry at Leeds University. We now meet regularly and she is part of the family again.

Me with my daughter Sonia

Olwen and I were married in September 2006, with Keith, my flying instructor, as best man, and with the blessing of her four sons, Anthony, Christopher, Timothy and Adrian, together with my own two sons, Michael and Peter.

Our wedding day, 8th September 2006

Olwen and her four sons, 8th September 2006

We sold our respective properties and bought a country house with eight acres, which we share with one horse, one donkey, one retired cow, one cat and two large Italian Spinone dogs which take me for a walk every day.

Our home

In the early 1970s, I had run into a period of financial difficulty and, as a result, I sold my flying Log Book and medals to a dealer; a decision I subsequently deeply regretted. When Olwen learned of this, she encouraged me to make an attempt to get my medals and Log Book back. The medals were a group of five, the Distinguished Flying Cross and Bar, the 1939–1945 Star, the Air Crew Europe Star with the France-Germany clasp, the Defence Medal, and the 1939–1945 War Medal. To trace my medals would be a very difficult task and, even if we found them, there was no guarantee that the new owner would agree to sell them back to me, nor indeed that they were still all together, but we could try and I could ask.

We wrote to every medal dealer and medal association in the UK, and eventually heard from a London dealer that my medals and Log Book had been sent from America to his London auction in 2000, when they had been sold to a dealer in

Canada. I telephoned Canada and spoke to the dealer but he could not, or would not, recall to whom he had subsequently sold them, which I found disappointing since I had imagined that dealers kept very detailed records for their own purposes. I advertised in American and Canadian medal society magazines, but all to no avail; the trail had gone cold. Several months later, out of the blue, we received a telephone call from a dealer in Bridlington, telling us to log on to the Internet. We did so and there on display were my medals and Log Book, shown by a collector, Nick de Carteret, in New Zealand.

There was an intense flurry of e-mails as I started to negotiate to buy back these items. Finally, Nick agreed to sell them to me for the price he had paid, plus carriage. Nick and I were strangers to one another, so there had to be an element of trust in the transaction. I took cash from my bank, crossed the road and paid it into a branch of a national bank which Nick used in the UK. He despatched the items via Fedex in Auckland on the Wednesday morning, and I received them in Shropshire that following Friday afternoon. I was overjoyed; everything was intact and just as I remembered them, despite the fact that they had travelled the globe in the intervening years. It was like meeting up with an old and dear friend again.

My medals, Log Book and Air Chief Marshal Harris's message have an immense sentimental value to me, and of course certainly have an intrinsic value too, but the even greater value is what they represent. They bear witness to a time when the fight to preserve our very existence as an independent nation consumed our every effort, when the whole nation really was all in it together, because losing was unthinkable. They represent not just a recognition of my own part in that struggle but also the incalculable sacrifice of so many who did not survive, some of them my close friends, and of those who did but bore the scars for the rest of their lives.

Johnnie Trotman, DFC & Bar

Later, Olwen and I planned a trip to New Zealand and we sent an e-mail to Nick saying that we would like to meet him and his wife at the Hermitage Hotel in Auckland. We received no reply, and assumed Nick had no wish to meet us. We stayed overnight at the Hermitage overlooking the harbour, then picked up a hire car and proceeded to explore North Island. Arriving at Paraparamui near Wellington, I decided to check my e-mails back in the UK. There was a message from Nick saying I had sent my e-mail to an address he seldom used, and that he and his wife had been sorry to miss us. Accordingly, I telephoned him and agreed we would continue our exploration of South Island, fly back from Christchurch to Auckland, and spend some time with them.

In South Island, as well as taking in the fabulous scenery, we took the opportunity of visiting the Wanaka Air Museum, largely dedicated to New Zealand fighter pilots in World War 2.

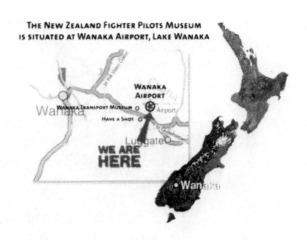

Wanaka Museum

Additionally, we took a flight in a ski plane and the pilot landed us on a glacier adjacent to Mount Cook. It was amazing to step out of the plane onto the snow and ice to view the wonderful scenery.

On Mount Cook

Back in Auckland, Nick invited us to stay in an apartment he rented in the Hermitage Hotel, and looking out of the window, we discovered the same view we had seen when staying at the hotel before. It then transpired that the night we had stayed at the Hermitage on our arrival in New Zealand, Nick had been staying in his apartment two floors below. We got to know Nick and his wife Jenny, and enjoyed our visit, which included seeing the Auckland Air Museum, before flying on to Sydney, San Francisco, New York and Washington.

Subsequently, Nick and Jenny came to England and stayed with us, and as Nick was very interested in World War Two memorabilia, I took the opportunity of flying him, Jenny and Olwen to RAF Cosford in a Club plane to view the Royal Air Force Museum there: it was a very enjoyable day.

In recent years, the RAF at Shawbury have been very kind to me, together with four other veterans, Allen Scott, Jim Penny, Ron Smyth, and Brian Beattie, giving us invitations to visit their Officers' Mess for dinners and Battle of Britain functions.

[l-r] Captain Shawcross, Brian Beattie, Alan Scott, Air Chief Marshal Peach, Ron Smyth, Mile Bailey, John Trotman, Group Captain Luck

We have also had invitations extended to us as members of the Air Crew Association. We were even given the opportunity to try our hand at flying the Griffin helicopter simulator. When I heard that this opportunity was to be presented to us, I sent for a book on how to fly helicopters. As a result, I had a very enjoyable half hour – and didn't 'crash' it.

Griffin helicopter [courtesy of RAF Shawbury]

Olwen and I continue to fly, and she has taken up training to be a safety pilot. This means that should I become incapacitated whilst flying, Olwen would be able to take over the aircraft and make a safe landing. This has meant converting to a Cessna C172 high-wing plane which we can both access with ease and safety.

One Sunday, we flew with Keith and his wife from the Flying Club at Sleap to Booker aerodrome at High Wycombe, where we were met by my eldest son, Michael, who took us to lunch in Marlow on the Thames, after which we flew back to Shropshire in time for tea; a very civilised way of travelling.

Another high point of my recent flying has been for me to have the opportunity of piloting a four-seater aircraft with state-of-the-art controls. The instrument panel consisted of two TV-type screens, one displaying the flight instruments and the other the engine instruments or navigation details, similar to commercial airlines.

File:Cirrus Interior.jpg

From Wikipedia, the free encyclopedia

Size of this preview: 800 × 600 pixels.
Full resolution (2,272 × 1,704 pixels, file size: 1.55 MB, MIME type: image/jpeg)

[courtesy Cirrus Aircraft/Wikipedia]

In 2008, Olwen and I made a trip to Canada, flying to Calgary, then driving up to Edmonton to visit friends, then on to Jasper, the Icefield Parkway, Banff, Vancouver and Vancouver Island. We returned to Banff and Calgary having driven almost 3,000 miles which we shared between us.

City of Calgary

In Calgary, we had been invited to attend the local Aircrew Association monthly luncheon at the Armoury, where I was asked to address the members, after which we flew to Regina, the home of the Mounties, and stayed with friends on a large ranch in Saskatchewan, before continuing to Toronto and Niagara Falls. We were fortunate in flying the leg Calgary – Regina – Toronto where we were assisted by an executive of Westjet airline who is an honorary member of the Calgary Air Crew Association.

We celebrated my 90th birthday on September 9th 2011 with a large party held at a local hotel, sent out invitations to 120 people, and everyone came and enjoyed themselves. The event opened with a very fine aerobatic display over the hotel by the Chief Flying Instructor, Bob Pooler from Sleap Flying Club. I had hoped to fly that day to celebrate the event, but unfortunately was unable to do so because of a hip problem.

In the early hours of the following morning, Olwen turned over in bed and dislocated her hip, necessitating my calling for an ambulance to take her to Shrewsbury Hospital. At 7am, I rang friends, who agreed to take care of the horse, the donkey, the dogs and the cat, because at 9am another friend was coming to take me to Oswestry Orthopaedic Hospital for my own hip replacement operation. For the rest of the week, Olwen and I were using our mobile phones to communicate with each other from our respective hospital beds!

In January 2012, I received a letter of invitation to attend the unveiling of the Bomber Command Memorial at Green Park in London on June 28th. Olwen and I naturally accepted the invitation to this important event, which was recognition at last, after nearly 70 years, of the immense sacrifices made by members of Bomber Command.

I immediately rang the RAF Club in London to get accommodation for us but they were already fully booked. I rang one or two London hotels to book a room but found that they had almost doubled their charges to take advantage of people attending the various forthcoming events of 2012, the Queen's Jubilee, the unveiling of the Bomber Command Memorial, tennis at Wimbledon, and the Olympics. I tried the Union Jack Club and was able to book a suite, which was all they had, but at a very reasonable price. In addition, we booked rail fares from Crewe to Euston, advance off-peak, with Railcards meaning we would travel First Class at less than the standard fare.

In February, I had my right hip replaced, followed by a hernia operation in April. I was joining the 'hippies' and getting my parts replaced bit by bit.

On 27th June we travelled to London and, on arrival at Euston, took advantage of the free facility of being met off the train and conveyed in a golf-type trolley to the front of the taxi rank. Later, we attended a reception at the City of London Guildhall held by the Lord Mayor to honour the veterans of Bomber Command. Present were a number of veterans not only from Britain but also from Australia, Canada and New Zealand. Sadly, I knew no-one there, all my old colleagues being long gone, so Olwen and I went round the Great Hall meeting and greeting as many veterans as we could from all countries. It was an emotional experience!

City of London Guildhall

The next morning, a taxi took us to Green Park for the Memorial unveiling. That day, the London taxi drivers very generously refused to accept any money from veterans, whether in fares or tips. In front of the actual Memorial there was seating for 1,000, which was for immediate relatives of the fallen, overseas veterans, and VIPs. Just behind the trees was a larger Salute Area with seating for 5,000 to which we had been directed. We arrived promptly at 9am and in fact we were the first people in this arena and were thus able to obtain a seat in the front row centre, in front of a large stage and giant TV screen, with an area in front of us reserved for wheelchair veterans and their carers.

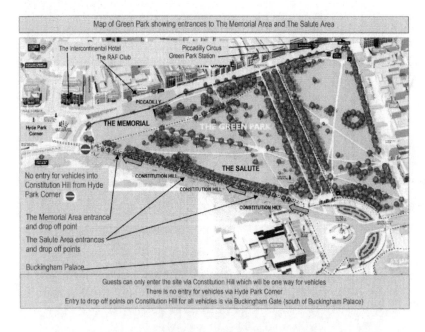

Green Park London

We were entertained by choirs and bands up to the time of the arrival at the Memorial of HM the Queen, Prince Philip and other members of the Royal Household. Thereafter, we joined in the Dedication service, which was deeply moving, at the conclusion of which PA474, the Lancaster Bomber of the Battle of Britain Memorial Flight, flew over, dropping 55,573 poppies. Unfortunately, the breeze took most into neighbouring Hyde Park and they had to be retrieved by the many ATC personnel present.

Thursday 28th June 2012.
Her Majesty The Queen unveiling the
Bomber Command Memorial

Courtesy Tim Clarke, Daily Express

28th June 2012

The weather was intensely hot, and after the service was over, Olwen and I found a position under some trees where we could cool off. We ended up on a broad footpath which led to the Memorial and were standing there when Prince Charles and Camilla arrived to shake hands with veterans.

Prince Charles greeting Veterans (Rear view of self)

After that, we walked up to the Memorial, which is a magnificent tribute to the 55,573 men of Bomber Command who had given their lives for our nation. It was also a tribute to the many people who had devoted so much time and effort to its creation, including Robin Gibb's determination, Liam O'Connor's architecture, and Philip Jackson's sculpture; a fitting memorial, which must be seen to be fully appreciated.

Bomber Command Memorial Figures

We thought that, as it was so hot, we would cross the road to the RAF Club to get a drink, but found this was not possible. Parked outside the Club was a large Rolls Royce flying the Royal Standard, along with a heavy police presence. We went back to the Union Jack Club.

The next day, Friday, we returned to Crewe, picked up our car and drove to York, where we stayed at a hotel we use when we are in the area. On Saturday, we attended the Mosquito Association reunion at Elvington Airfield Museum and spent the day meeting other members, including two from New Zealand who were involved in building a Mosquito at Ardmore on North Island, which was scheduled to fly in September. The Museum had gone to a great deal of trouble to refurbish a non-flying Mosquito for the occasion of our visit.

Comrades
[Photo courtesy of support@newsprints.co.uk]

On Sunday 1st July, we returned home, and then on Monday went back to London as we had been invited, along with four other veterans, to a dinner hosted by the All Party Parliamentary Group for the Armed Forces at the Terrace Restaurant in the House of Commons. Present were Members from the House of Lords and the House of Commons, several Air Marshals, one or two researchers and a representative from Boeing Aircraft.

House of Commons

The other four veterans were Harry Irons DFC, Harry Hughes DFC, DFM, John Banfield MBE, all three of whom had been featured in Bomber Command television programmes and books, and an Australian veteran, Bill McFadden DFM from Sydney. The food was good, a speech was made by Air Chief Marshal Sir Glen Torpy, and a reply was given by an MP. I asked if I might speak on behalf of the veterans and this was agreed.

ALL-PARTY PARLIAMENTARY GROUP FOR THE ARMED FORCES

Bomber Command celebration dinner 2nd July 2012 TABLE PLAN

DOOR END CORRIDOR SIDE

	Seb	Cox
	Jack	Lopresti MP
	Dean	Benton
	Oliver	Colvile MP
	Gerry	McFall
	Tobias	Ellwood MP
	Harry	Hughes DFC, DFM
	Mark	Francois MP
Air Chief Marshal Sir	Glen	Torpy
Sir	Roger	Gale MP
Air Cdre	Charles	Clarke OBE
Rt Hon Dr Lord (John)		Gilbert
	Harry	Irons DFC
Rt Hon	Anne	McGuire MP
	Roger	Bennett
Rt Hon	Bob	Ainsworth MP
	John	Banfield MBE
Lord	(Denis)	Rogan
DOOR SIDE		
FAR END		
WINDOW SIDE		
	Ian	Murray MP
	Cliff	Waldwyn
Baroness	(Angela)	Harris of Richmond
	David	Clelland-Smith
Lord	(John)	Lee of Trafford DL
	David	Wilby
Rt Hon Lord	(Tommy)	McAvoy
	Robin	Ashby
	Emma	Dove
	Madeline	Moon MP
Air Marshal Sir	Rob	Wright
	James	Gray MP
	Bill	McFadden DFM
	Meredith	McFadden
	Olwen	Dickenson
	John	Trotman DFC*
	Michael	Holden
Sir	Bob	Russell MP

DOOR END WINDOW SIDE

To promote in Parliament better understanding of the UK's armed forces, and their objectives and activitie

Officers 2011 - 2012: James Gray MP (Chairman); Chris Bryant MP (Deputy Chairman); Lord Lee of Trafford DL (Deputy Chairman); Angu Robertson MP (Deputy Chairman); Caroline Dinenage MP (Vice Chairman Royal Navy); Oliver Colvile MP (Vice Chairman Royal Marines) Madeleine Moon MP (Vice Chairman RAF); Bob Stewart DSO, MP (Vice Chairman Army); Lord Moonie (Co-Treasurer); Mark Pritchard MP (Co-Treasurer); Jonathan Reynolds MP (Secretary).

The other three Veterans were two who had been featured in Bomber Command TV programmes and books, and an Australian Veteran from Sydney. The food was good , a speech was made by Air Chief

Guest List

I thanked them for their hospitality, reviewed our visit to the Guildhall, referred to the unveiling of the Memorial by HM the Queen, and the fact that at last recognition had been given to the men of Bomber Command. I referred to the loss of 55,573 lives by men who had fought Nazi tyranny to protect the freedom and independence of our nation. Unfortunately, in the post-war period, Edward Heath had turned his back on the Commonwealth and taken our country into the Common Market, now the EU, where we had lost the freedom and independence for which those men gave so much. I moved on to the need to get our freedom and independence back and get out of Europe politically but remain in for trade, and to achieve this through a national referendum. As a guest at the dinner, I was probably speaking out of turn, but frankly I didn't care, these things had to be said. Amazingly, I got some applause, and some MPs came to me afterwards and said how much they agreed with my sentiments

I have said many times that, in this life, you never know what is around the next corner. In May 2013, I received an e-mail from a friend, Dave, indicating that Blast Films were making a film featuring the Mosquito aircraft. It was suggested I get in touch with Blast Films, which I understood were very interested in including me in the film. Accordingly, I contacted them, agreed to participate, and subsequently met the film crew at the Shropshire Aero Club at Sleap. I was asked to fly a Cessna C172, taking off and landing it twice, and was then interviewed in a hangar by Arthur Williams, a truly remarkable young man.

John Trotman

The programme, called 'The Plane that saved Britain', was shown on Channel 4 and Channel 47 in July, and covered the many parts that the Mosquito aircraft played during World War Two.

THE PLANE THAT SAVED BRITAI
SUNDAY 21ST JULY 8PM ON CHANNEL 4

rthur Williams presents this love letter
the Second World War aeroplane he
elieves history has unjustly forgotten.
A terrific film'
RADIO TIMES

PRESENTER
Arthur Williams

PRODUCTION MANAGER
Michelle Galvin

EXECUTIVE PRODUC
Alistair Pegg

st! films for 4

EDITOR
Mike Burton

PRODUCER/DIRECT
Rob Coldstream

Arthur Williams

In subsequent conversations with people who saw the film, I was surprised how little appreciation there was of this outstanding aeroplane by the general public. They knew all about Hurricanes, Spitfires and Lancasters, but little about the Mosquito. The film opened their eyes.

In February 2014, along with Jim Penny and Keith Martin, I was presented with the Bomber Command Clasp by Air Marshal Baz North at Shawbury.

Air Marshal Baz North – and me [courtesy RAF Shawbury]

And so my life, with all its ups and downs, has been good to me, and I thank God for my good health and good fortune. I am grateful for the friendship, comradeship and help given me over the years by colleagues and friends. I hope that when the day of reckoning comes, I may be forgiven for causing the deaths of so many people during the war, and given credit for some of the good things I have done in my life since. I have a large family around me, and I am grateful for having met and fallen in love, late in life, with Olwen, who gives me much comfort and support, loves me, and keeps me young.

'For Johnnie'

Do not despair
For Johnnie-head-in-air
He sleeps as sound
As Johnnie underground.
Fetch out no shroud
For Johnnie-in-the-cloud;
And keep your tears
For him in after years
Better by far
For Johnnie-the-bright-star
To keep your head
And see his children fed.

John Pudney.

Appendix – My 'Lost' Medals

When conducting the search for my medals, I eventually found them for sale, described as follows, along with the relevant citations from the *London Gazette*:

Groups and Single Decorations for Gallantry
A fine Second War Mosquito Pilot's D.F.C. and Bar
Group of five awarded to Flight Lieutenant P.J.P.
Trotman, Nos 150 and 692 Squadrons, Royal Air Force.
Distinguished Flying Cross, G.V1.R, with Second
Award Bar, the reverse of both officially dated 1945;
1939-45 Star; Air Crew Europe Star; Defence & War
Medals, mounted as worn, together with his two
Pilots Flying Log Books for the period November 1940
to March 1946, handsomely bound as one in blue cloth
embossed with his name and containing several
photographs and a congratulatory telegram from
'Bomber Harris', nearly extremely fine (5) £1400-1800.

D.F.C. *London Gazette* 13 February 1945: 'One night in December, 1944, Flying Officer Trotman was captain of an aircraft detailed to attack Ludwigshafen. Shortly after leaving the target area, the starboard engine failed and soon after the port engine became defective and lost power considerable height was lost and it seemed as though the aircraft would have to be abandoned. The defective port engine suddenly resumed full power, however, and Flying Officer Trotman flew the aircraft to an airfield in France where he executed a safe landing with the undercarriage retracted. This officer had displayed commendable gallantry, and outstanding skill, and has at all times proved himself a cool and resolute captain.'

Bar to D.F.C. *London Gazette* 26 October 1945. The following details are taken from the original recommendation for the award of the Bar:

'Flight Lieutenant Trotman has participated in numerous sorties since the award of the Distinguished Flying Cross. He has completed a second tour of operations against heavily defended targets in Germany including 19 attacks against Berlin. At all times he has set an inspiring example.'

NB. The actual detailed facts relating to the award of the original DFC are contained in this book in the chapter covering the Second Tour. JT.